Co-parenting by Design

THE DEFINITIVE GUIDE FOR DIVORCED OR SEPARATED PARENTS

ANNETTE T. BURNS, JD

NICOLE SIQUEIROS-STOUTNER, JD

UNHOOKED BOOKS
Independent Publishers since 2011
an imprint of High Conflict Institute Press
Scottsdale, Arizona

Testimonials

"This book hit me deeply as a single mother who has walked through the pain of a traumatic divorce and witnessed firsthand the profound impact it had on my two boys. With the wisdom and compassion of a family law lawyer, it reminds us that healthy co-parenting isn't just a hopeful ideal—it's a lifeline for our children's emotional well-being. Through every page, the author's insights resonated with my own struggles and reaffirmed the critical importance of setting aside conflict to build a foundation of support for our kids. The truth is, the way we choose to co-parent will shape their healing and their ability to navigate relationships in the future. For any parent facing this journey, this book is a powerful reminder that our children's hearts deserve the greatest care, even when our own are breaking."

—**JAMIE KING**, mother, filmmaker, actress

"In *Co-Parenting by Design*, Annette and Nicole have defined and described the realities of co-parenting—with all its ups and downs—in detail, as only experienced family lawyers can do (60 years between them!). They explain common difficulties on up to the extreme behaviors of child abuse, domestic violence, and parental alienation. Then, they go into great detail about what to do in every possible conflict situation, including the use of parallel parenting, managed emails (including the BIFF method, of course), and parenting schedules. In addition, there is sample language that they offer which can be included in parenting plans. I do a lot of consultations with parents involved in high conflict cases and they often ask for specific language they can use in their agreements or proposed court orders. Coming from these experienced family lawyers, these sample paragraphs are a very useful add-on in making the book highly practical—and helpful in reducing conflict. Another plus is the detailed list of resources at the end, which will save readers a lot of research. I will be recommending this book to many of my consultation clients."

—**BILL EDDY**, LCSW, JD, family therapist, lawyer, mediator, and co-author of *BIFF for CoParent Communication,* developer of the New Ways for Families® parent skills training method, and co-founder of the High Conflict Institute.

"A tremendously useful book, *Co-parenting by Design* delivers practical strategies, evidence-based advice (including references), and word-for-word clauses that can be used in co-parenting plans and similar documents and agreements. The authors, seasoned family law attorneys, speak with realism and reassurance. They give us ample down-to-earth examples of how their specific solutions effectively reduce and prevent conflict and stress. Written for divorcing parents who range from co-operative to high-conflict, at a critical juncture in their child-rearing, this book opens doors for their children to thrive."

 —**LUCY JO PALLADINO**, PhD, Clinical Psychologist & Author, *Parenting in the Age of Attention Snatchers*

"Our job as parents is to provide our children with a safety net so that they can grow and learn and explore without fear of falling. Adult conflict, separation, and divorce can create gaping holes in that safety net, imperiling our kids. *Co-parenting By Design* is 214 pages of expert, practical, down-to-earth advice that helps us all keep our kids' safety net intact even while we renegotiate our adult relationships. Thank you, attorneys Burns and Siqueiros-Stoutner for showing us how to keep our children's needs first!

 —**BENJAMIN D. GARBER**, PhD, author, *Mending Fences; High-Conflict Litigation;* and co-sponsor of DefuseDivorce.com

"*Co-Parenting By Design* is a comprehensive and well-documented, but totally understandable plan for parents trying to navigate life post-separation. There are scores of suggestions for both the most common and the most unusual parenting issues. Burns and Siqueiros-Stoutner have addressed every potential area of dispute. Most family law litigation involves at least one and often two, self-represented litigants. Many have limited resources and are left to manage court and post-court issues on their own. This book will be especially helpful for them. Parents can readily access the many examples, templates and resources. If *Co-Parenting by Design* had been available when I was on the family law bench, I would have recommended it in every case involving children."

 —**KAREN S. ADAM**, Superior Court Judge (Ret.)

"I wholeheartedly recommend *Co-Parenting By Design*. It is an invaluable resource that equips professionals and parents with practical tools and expert advice to make the challenging co-parenting experience smoother and more effective. The inclusion of sample parenting plan language is particularly helpful for dealing with today's issues, such as social media, technology and parallel parenting, and for reducing conflict and misunderstanding.

This book has a strong foundation in research, addressing the complexities of parenting plans with a focus on the best interests of the children. By prioritizing children's needs and fostering cooperative communication, *Co-Parenting By Design* empowers parents to navigate conflict and create a nurturing environment. This is a "must have" resource for every professional (and any parent) seeking to enhance the co-parenting experience."

—**BETHANY HICKS**, Superior Court Judge (Ret.)

Publisher's Note

This publication is designed to provide accurate and authoritative information about the subject matters covered. It is sold with the understanding that neither the authors nor publisher are rendering legal, mental health, or other professional services, either directly or indirectly. If expert assistance, legal services, or counseling is needed, the services of a competent professional should be sought. Neither the authors nor the publisher shall be liable or responsible for any loss or damage allegedly arising as a consequence of your use or application of any information or suggestions in this book.

Copyright © 2024 by Annette T. Burns, Nicole Siqueiros-Stoutner

All rights reserved
Printed in the United States of America
First Edition
For information about permission to reproduce selections from this book, write to info@unhookedbooks.com or use the Contact Form at www.unhookedbooks.com.

Cover design by Julian León, The Missive
Interior Design by Jeffrey Fuller, Shelfish

ISBN (print): 978-1950057429
ISBN (eBook): 978-1950057436
Library of Congress Control Number: 2024942736

Unhooked Media, 7701 E. Indian School Rd., Ste. F, Scottsdale, AZ 85251
www.unhookedmedia.com

Dedication

This book is dedicated to my children, who were my original parenting guides, and I now have the pleasure of seeing firsthand the amazing parents they've become.

—Annette

To my daughter, who is my heart and teaches me about parenting every day.

—Nicole

Contents

Introduction i

PART 1: CO-PARENTING AND ITS CHALLENGES 1

Chapter 1: Co-parenting 3
    A. How Do "Good Enough" Co-parents Work? 4
    B. Accepting Differences and Ending Competition 5
    C. Parent Education Required by the Court 6
    D. Parenting Coordination 7

Chapter 2: Obstacles to Co-parenting 10
    A. Poor Parent Communication. 12
    B. Gatekeeping Issues 12
    C. Exposing the Child to Parental Conflict. 14
    D. Parent-Child Contact Problems and "Alienation" 16
    E. Personality Disorders and Mental Health Issues 19
    F. Substance Abuse of a Parent. 20
    G. Domestic Violence 21
    H. How Ineffective Co-parenting Harms Children. 22

Chapter 3: Parallel Parenting: Is It a Solution? 24
    A. Key Concepts of Parallel Parenting. 25
    B. Using a Parenting Coordinator Can Support Parallel Parenting 28
    C. Implementing Parallel Parenting Concepts in your Parenting Plan . . . 29

Chapter 4: Communicating with Your Co-parent 32
    A. Using this Book with Your Co-parent 32
    B. Less Blame, More Respect. 33
    C. Choosing and Using the Right Communication 34
    D. Keep It Brief, Informative, Friendly, and Firm 38
    E. More Tips for Writing Effective Emails 40
    F. Apps for Communication Between Parents. 45
    G. Don't Use the Child to Communicate 46

**PART 2: SAMPLE SOLUTIONS AND LANGUAGE
FOR SPECIFIC SITUATIONS** 49

Chapter 5: Time Sharing/Parenting Time 51

   A. Residential Care: The Standard Parenting Schedule 51

   B. Infant and Toddler Parenting Time 55

   C. Should the Child Be Interviewed? 57

   D. Equal Time? 58

   E. Using an Online Calendar 59

   F. Working Parents and Childcare Considerations....................... 60

   G. Childcare and Caretakers 60

   H. When the Child Is Sick 60

   I. Holidays, Vacations, and Special Days 61

   J. Transitions (Exchanges) and Transportation 73

   K. Travel with the Child.. 80

   L. First Right of Refusal... 89

Chapter 6: Telephone Calls Between Child and Parent 93

   A. Types of Contact 94

   B. Frequency of Contact 95

   C. Environment for Child's Telephone and Facetime Calls 96

   D. Important Guidelines for Parents....................................... 97

   E. A Sample (very specific) Phone Call Clause 97

   F. Parent Child Interactions at Special Events 98

Chapter 7: Child Medical Care Decisions............................... 100

   A. Routine Medical Care, Check-Ups, and Scheduling Appointments...102

   B. Child Therapy and Parents' Participation.............................106

   C. Safe Haven Counseling for a Child.................................... 110

Chapter 8: Safety Decisions 114

   A. Car Seats 114

   B. Swimming Pools.. 115

   C. Trampolines and other "Dangerous" Activities....................... 115

   D. Child Walking to School..117

   E. Motorcycles and Off-Road Motorized Vehicles 117

   F. Child as Babysitter 118

   G. Unsafe Pets 120

   H. Covid and the Pandemic 120

Chapter 9: Educational Decisions 122

   A. School Enrollment and Decisions...................................... 123

   B. Access to School Information and Homework 124

   C. Kindergarten and Elementary School 125

   D. Parent-Teacher Conferences 127

   E. Transition from Middle School to High School 128

   F. One Parent's Desire to Change Schools.............................. 128

   G. Parents Living a Substantial Distance Apart 129

   H. Parenting Time and Presence at School 130

   I. Testing.. 132

   J. Notices of Education Issues 132

   K. School Absences and Tardies... 133

   L. The Exceptional Child 136

Chapter 10: Extracurricular Decisions 143

   A. Concerns about Parenting Time....................................... 144

   B. Legitimate Disagreement about what Activity is Best 145

   C. Agreement to an Activity: Notice and Information 147

   D. Who Attends the Activities 148

   E. Payment for Activities 150

Chapter 11: Child's Possessions 151

   A. Electronics Including Phones 151

   B. The "Wubby" 153

   C. Clothing, Shoes... 153

   D. Special Events and Sports Gear 155

   E. Forgotten Items 156

   F. Child's Legal Paperwork 157

Chapter 12: Personal Care Decisions 158

   A. What Is a Routine Decision? 158

   B. Temporary versus Permanent Decision 159

   C. Are Religious Decisions Routine?. 160

Chapter 13: Child's Social Media and Device Use. 162

   A. Online Safety 163

   B. Access to the Child's Online Accounts. 164

   C. Privacy. 164

Chapter 14: Driver's License and Driver Education. 167

Chapter 15: Special Circumstances 170

   A. Relocation 170

   B. Long Distance Parenting Time. 172

   C. Parent Child Contact Problems (PCCP) 177

   D. Domestic Violence 177

   E. Substance Abuse of a Parent 179

   F. Supervised Parenting Time 182

Chapter 16: Reimbursement of Expenses 185

Chapter 17: Dispute Resolution. 191

   Appendix 1: Abbreviations 194

   Appendix 2: Recommended Reading, Apps, and Websites 195

   Appendix 3: Sample Holiday Plan Chart 201

   Appendix 4: Sample Technology Agreement. 204

Notes. 206

Acknowledgments 210

The Authors. 213

Introduction

Why was this book written? It is written for those of you who want to co-parent better, who wonder if you're the problem, or who are pretty sure the other parent is the problem, but you still want to make things better. It's for those of you who need better boundaries in their co-parenting documents (also called Parenting Plans or Court Orders). It's for attorneys who would like a deeper dive into specific problems that come up in parenting agreements and who don't want to re-invent all the best solutions or clauses for their clients. And it's for those of you who are stuck with boilerplate forms and clauses that just don't work for your parenting situation.

Part One doesn't focus on the Plan documents or phrases. It focuses on the co-parenting relationship, what can be wrong about it and what can be done to improve it, and why the co-parenting relationship should be improved if at all possible. Ideally, after understanding how important that relationship is, you can move into Part Two and work with your co-parent to improve your Parenting Plan for everyone's sake.

One important note: this is not a book about how to parent your child.

There are plenty of parenting books and resources on the market. This book focuses on YOU and your co-parent. The better you work things out, the more your child benefits!

From Author Annette

Divorced and separated parents are expected to be superhuman. They are expected to forget and forgive past transgressions, have unending patience, be perfect in their parenting and their interactions with the other parent, never forget anything, and be kind and compassionate, no matter the circumstances.

None of those expectations are reasonable. Parents are under a great deal of stress, feeling that they're constantly scrutinized (by the other parent and by the court system) to meet these unreasonable standards. If you are a divorced or separated parent, you may be feeling the burden of such stress and expectations.

How can this book help? This book is an effort to show you that you're not alone, that expectations can be adjusted, and with the help of reasonable Parenting Plan orders, good communication, and common sense, you can do your best at co-parenting with less trauma and drama. This will cause less stress and more free time to spend with your child.

Parenting Plan orders (hereafter referred to as "Plan") are orders entered by the court in your divorce or paternity case. They may be something you and your co-parent agreed to and signed. Some parents are able to create a Plan on their own, or they may use lawyers or mediators to help them create it. We strongly suggest having either a lawyer or mediator who knows about Parenting Plans. Review your Plan to see that everything is covered, but if you use the suggestions in this book, you'll be well on your way to having a complete Plan. If you and your co-parent can't agree on things, there will be decisions made by the court about your Plan. Either way, the Parenting Plan needs to be in writing.

This book will help you and your child's other parent in developing a Parenting Plan. Or, if you already have a Parenting Plan, this book will help you figure out what your Plan is missing or what needs to be changed about it. In Part 1, we cover the ins and outs of effective co-parenting including using parallel parenting to reduce conflict. In Part 2, we discuss specific disputes and give you proposed language that works to address and resolve co-parenting concerns and conflicts.

While child-related research supports what's written here, this book is not intended to be a volume of research. It is intended as an operating manual and is based on the authors' combined 60+ years of experience in family law as lawyers, judicial officers, and mediators.

The main thing we authors hope you will do after reading this book is adjust your expectations. Parents often have unreasonable expectations for themselves and for the other parent and for what the court can do to help them. The best thing parents can do to resolve co-parenting difficulties with the other person is to work them out, and this book offers ways to try to do that.

In an ideal world, two co-parents would read this book and implement suggestions together. While it's sometimes not easy to accept solutions offered by the other parent, taking suggestions from neutral third parties (such as these authors) might be easier. Assuming only one parent in a family is reading this book, and there's not much likelihood of the other parent reading it, the parent who is reading it can still put some of these suggestions into practice. "I think we should talk about this . . . What if we agreed to do that? . . . Can we add a provision that makes it clear when we exchange Ethan during Christmas break?" We're trying to help co-parents think of problem areas with their Parenting Plan and get those areas fixed before it's an emergency or a last-minute issue.

Finally, our suggestions (Part 2) on how to handle certain situations are just that: suggestions. Not everyone will agree with the way we suggest things. The point of our suggestions is to make you think about how different ways of handling things will affect your child and affect the co-parenting relationship. In several areas, we've added "consider both sides" arguments to discuss why there is more than one way to address a situation.

From Author Nicole

Every parent I know acknowledges the demanding nature of the role. I often joke that my daughter would owe me millions of dollars if I billed her by the hour for the time I spent parenting her! Parents spend so much time fulfilling their child's needs, such as food, clothing, etc. They invest time in education, activities, and transportation. Given the changing nature of children, parents also devote significant time to strategic planning for their child's future and addressing emerging issues.

When I reflect on the effort needed to foster the well-being of a child in our modern world, it's clear that parents need to find some way to work together in order to support their children and meet their many needs. Everyone suffers, especially children, if parents cannot be effective co-parents.

When my parents were growing up in the 1950s, the common belief was that parents must stay in an intact family at least until a child graduates from high school because divorce itself will harm the children. That isn't true.

Since the 1950s, a great deal of research shows that children are harmed when they are exposed to their parents' conflict, regardless of whether they are in an intact family or a divorced/separated family. The legal status of the parents' relationship is not as significant as what the child experiences. Children who are subjected to ongoing parental disputes, poor co-parenting, ineffective communication, and the like experience long-term social, academic, medical, and psychological issues. However, learning how to eliminate or reduce this conflict and navigating parenting relationships, especially the complex dynamic that comes with parenting after divorce or separation, is not something we are born to do; it is not innate.

As a separated or divorced parent, you must actively learn the skills necessary to have a healthy functioning relationship with your co-parent. This book is designed to teach you how to do that and provide you with strategies you can implement to improve yourself and your co-parenting relationship.

This process is not easy. I encourage you to be patient with both yourself and your co-parent. Remember, co-parenting requires time and perseverance. Practice self-forgiveness when you fall short of your best self and extend that same forgiveness to your co-parent. Finally, cultivate a level of empathy for your co-parent, recognizing that their struggles are just as challenging as your own, even if they are not always obvious to you.

Most importantly, striving to be the best co-parent you can be creates an environment where your child can thrive and reach their full potential—a goal every caring parent desires.

PART 1

CO-PARENTING AND
ITS CHALLENGES

Co-parenting when you are separated or divorced isn't easy, but it is possible. In Part 1, we explain what co-parenting is, what makes it challenging, and how to do it with less conflict between you and your co-parent. The goals are prioritizing your child and minimizing any harmful effects on your child, which results in more peace of mind for you.

Throughout this book, we refer to just "the child," but suggestions apply to families with two or more children as well. We may refer to the child as "him" or "her" as examples, but that's for convenience, and all suggestions apply to a child of either gender. If we ever refer to a parent as "him" or "her," or father or mother, that's done simply for convenience and not because fathers or mothers are more likely to cause a particular problem, nor are we ignoring the fact that not all co-parenting relationships are opposite sex. Every co-parenting issue we've dealt with in our combined sixty years of family law practice originates from both parents, regardless of gender, regardless of economic or social status, and regardless of age.

CHAPTER ONE

Co-parenting

People divorce or separate for various reasons. But if they have children, they continue to be forced into a relationship. That relationship is called co-parenting. Co-parenting can be defined as the collaboration in child-drearing of two parents who share the responsibilities for at least one child.[1] Co-parenting involves interactions between parents about their child. It does not include aspects of their relationship that aren't about the child (such as their romantic, financial, or legal relationships).

Parents may make whatever they want out of their co-parenting relationship, but the relationship will only rise to the level of the parent with the lower standards, the lesser conduct, and the weaker principles for the relationship. No matter how hard one person tries, one person alone can't make a good two-person relationship. Effective co-parenting involves some level of joint effort between the adults. While you may not like the other parent and working with them may be difficult, co-parents are better when they find a way to reduce conflict, present themselves to the children in solidarity, and display a mutual level of respect.

Like just about anything else in life, co-parenting can be done skillfully or unskillfully. If every parent followed the Co-parenting Bill of Rights below, this book wouldn't be necessary.:

- Every child has a right to a meaningful relationship with each parent.

- Every child has a right not to be caught in the middle of parental conflict.

- Every parent has a right to have a meaningful relationship with their child without the interference of the other parent.

Since the need to co-parent arises because a relationship is ending or at least going through a major transition, it's very normal for co-parents to get off to a rough start. Fortunately, things usually get easier with time. Studies have found that for most parents, the initial impairment to their ability to communicate and effectively co-parent resolves within 2-3 years following separation/divorce, and some form of functional co-parenting takes effect after that period.[2] Only the smallest percentage (approximately 10-15%) of co-parenting relationships remain in the high conflict and high engagement category after the transitional period of separation and/or divorce. The remainder of co-parenting relationships resolve as low conflict/low engagement (also known as parallel parenting), manageable conflict with low engagement, or low conflict/ high engagement, which describes the parents who are cooperative with each other.[3] With intention, effort, time, and a bit of luck, you will most likely find yourself in one of these categories.

A. How Do "Good Enough" Co-parents Work?

The popular perception is that the only way to have a healthy productive co-parenting relationship is for parents to resolve disputes immediately by working cooperatively and collaboratively, consistently supporting each other as friends, considering each other, communicating frequently and regularly, and being endlessly flexible with each other. But this sort of "ideal" co-parenting is probably rare, and co-parenting will vary vastly depending on each family's dynamic and needs.

In truth, most co-parents have found a way to collaborate in raising their child, although they may not be functioning in what is considered the "ideal" co-parenting dynamic. For instance, they may not communicate every day or follow the Parenting Plan to a "T." They may have disagreements and must employ various tools to resolve conflict, such as mediation. However, this can work too! Their children can be just as happy, healthy, and well-adjusted as the children of parents who are engaged in more interactive "ideal" co-parenting.

Ultimately, the effectiveness of co-parenting is gauged by its impact on the well-being of the child involved. Have the co-parents found a way to successfully establish strategies that minimize or eliminate any detrimental effects of their co-parenting style on their child? Perfection should not be your goal.

B. Accepting Differences and Ending Competition

You may feel that your co-parent needs to be "fixed" and made a better parent through education or training. It's important to remember that if the court orders give both parents specific parenting time with the child and joint custody or decision-making, the court has made an implicit finding that the parents are each "fit" to make decisions and care for the child during that person's parenting time. When the court finds a parent to be "unfit," it's likely that some form of supervised or limited parenting time will typically be ordered.

A court finding that the other parent is "fit" is a concept that's difficult for some parents to accept. You may read this and think, "There's no way that they are a fit parent!" You may find it easy to list all the ways the other parent is deficient in caring for your child. But, for better or for worse, your co-parent is probably not unfit in the legal sense. The words "competent," "minimally competent," or "adequate" could be substituted for "fit." The point is that this term is used when court orders have found that each parent is capable of caring for the child during his or her own time. Co-parents shouldn't try to "fix" the other parent; in fact, you will need to accept that your co-parent's standards for parenting may not be, and do not need to be, identical to yours. Practice acceptance in your interactions with your co-parent.

You must fundamentally accept that you cannot and will not engage, discipline, and interact with your child in exactly the same way as the other parent. It is okay if two parents are different and parent differently. Your child is going to be just fine if you allow the child to clean their room once a week when the other parent requires daily room cleaning.

Each parent brings a unique approach, shaped by their own experiences, values, and personalities, to parenting. Embrace diversity in parenting styles and recognize that each parent offers a distinctive and important benefit to the child. Try to appreciate the good the other parent brings to the table. Your child is strengthened when they have different environments and parental relationships. It broadens your child's perspective and equips them with a versatile set of skills to approach and adapt to life. Exposure to diverse parenting styles fosters adaptability, empathy, and a broader understanding of various communication and problem-solving techniques in children. Simply put, healthy, happy children are capable of being parented in two different households and by two different parents.

Finally, remember that parenting is not a competition. There are no winners or losers between parents. You will be a better parent when you resist vying for your child's affection and trying to outdo the other parent. Allow each other to raise the child in their own way and do not compare or compete.

C. Parent Education Required by the Court

At some point in your court process and creating a Parenting Plan, you may be told that it's required for you to go through a "parent education" or "parent information" course. The great majority of states in the U.S. require some form of parent education during a divorce or custody action, but the quality of the programs and content varies widely. This is not a course in how to parent but is designed to familiarize the parents with how their separation or divorce affects their child and, in particular, how their conflict affects their child.

Most parent education courses encourage parents to minimize conflict between each other and offer some strategies to minimize conflict. Some of the subjects discussed will be how to resolve time-sharing (and possibly child support) disputes, communication strategies with the other parent, experiences and problems to be expected during the separation, emotional concerns and needs of the child, and discussion of skills necessary to co-parent. The classes are usually offered online or virtually, and in most cases, the parents must file a certificate proving they completed the course.

These types of courses provide you with a very brief introduction to some of the challenges parents will face in navigating co-parenting after a divorce or separation. Even the parents who adopt many of the course concepts will find that co-parenting is difficult and that the course only scratches the surface of co-parenting issues. This is because they simply do not provide sufficient tools and resources to effectively co-parent. Parents are then left to teach themselves to effectively co-parent (many times by trial and error) or to rely on the court, lawyers, or parenting coordinators to help them communicate and resolve disputes. You can use this book as a resource to enhance the information provided in these classes.

D. Parenting Coordination

Parenting coordination is a process designed to assist separated and/or divorced parents who have not been able to successfully co-parent and who may have ongoing co-parenting conflict. A Parenting Coordinator (PC) is a trained and (almost always) court-appointed professional who aids parents in resolving their co-parenting disputes. PCs have expertise in helping co-parents in conflict. The PC's role is to help parents create a healthy and safe environment for their children, follow the court-ordered Parenting Plan, and facilitate productive communication.

The parenting coordination process is different depending on what jurisdiction is involved, and parameters for the use of a PC are usually established by statute, legislation, or court rule.[4] In addition, each jurisdiction varies as to whether parenting coordination may be ordered by the court without the parents' consent or at the request of only one parent, and in some jurisdictions, parenting coordination is available only through consent and stipulation of both parents. Different jurisdictions have different versions of what a PC can do. Depending where you live, the PC might have greater or lesser authority and may only be able to work with the parents to reach agreements rather than make decisions for the parents.[5-]

In Arizona and some other jurisdictions, a PC may make decisions similar to an arbitrator. Those decisions are then made part of your court orders and become part of your Parenting Plan. Examples of issues addressed by PCs in Arizona may include:

- Whether to register a child in extra-curricular activities, lessons, sports, and tutoring.
- Creating guidelines for parent engagement (and disengagement) and communication.
- The method and frequency for sharing child-related information.
- Managing clothing and belongings between two homes.
- Planning around vacation schedules.
- Handling conflicts or confusion regarding holidays and other temporary changes to routine parenting time.
- Addressing telephone/video contact between the child and a parent.
- Arranging and scheduling transportation and exchanges, as well as implementing rules for parental conduct during transitions.
- Scheduling of medical and other appointments for the child.
- Permitting temporary and minor adjustments to the parenting time schedule.
- Implementing rules for a child's social media and device use.

One of the most valuable things a PC can help parents do is to figure out how to resolve their conflicts on their own. PCs should not be appointed for years and years. One goal of a PC is to not be necessary anymore once the parents have seen how conflicts are resolved and how they can disengage from each other and from conflict.

This book will incorporate concepts often used by PCs (as well as by us when we have been PCs) that have been effective for families in conflict. Much of what PCs do can be accomplished by you and your co-parent through a carefully crafted Parenting Plan and by implementing the suggestions in this book.

CHAPTER TWO

Obstacles to Co-parenting

Even under the best of circumstances, co-parenting is not easy, and for any number of reasons people may co-parent ineffectively. Ineffective co-parenting refers to situations in which separated or divorced parents are unable to work together to raise their child. It may involve a lack of communication, collaboration, and shared decision-making between parents, which is likely resulting in negative effects on the well-being and development of their child.

The following are just a few examples of poor co-parenting and the consequences for the child.

- Parents cannot agree on who will be the child's dentist, so the child waits weeks in pain without dental care while the parents argue over the provider.

- At child exchanges, the parents engage in name-calling or become physical with each other while talking about each parent's new significant other. As a result, the child develops anxiety about exchanges, mistrusts their parents' new partners, and begins to name-call and hit a younger sibling.

- A parent sends over a dozen text messages a day to the other parent asking the same child-related question because they have not received an answer. The other parent is so overwhelmed or annoyed by the tremendous number of texts that they continue to be non-responsive, and the question posed by the texting parent goes unanswered. Both parents are so angry or stressed about the constant emailing that the child knows something is wrong and believes it to be their fault.

- One parent fails to include or notify the other parent about a meeting with the child's teacher. At the meeting, the teacher gives important information about the child's schoolwork and offers helpful information and tools to support the child in school. The parent who wasn't told about the meeting doesn't know of the problem and fails to give the child the support they need.

- One parent tells the child intimate details about the parents' relationship, including telling the child about all the money the other parent wasted and spent. This parent tells the child to watch for and report the other parent's expenses because so much money is wasted. The child then becomes a spy and aligns with the parent who made the accusation of wasted money. The child starts to mistrust one parent and becomes anxious that the family will run out of money.

- Because the parents don't speak with each other, a parent fails to follow the Parenting Plan on a holiday, either by refusing to return the child or not taking the parenting time the child was entitled to. This creates anxiety and confusion for the child as they don't know what the schedule is or when they will see one of their parents again.

There are many contributing factors that lead to ineffective co-parenting, like the examples described above. This chapter will address some of the worst situations that lead to long-term problems for the child.

A. Poor Parent Communication

The way parents communicate with each other, or don't, can negatively affect co-parenting. Co-parents may have various types of ineffective communication styles. Generally, when co-parents allow their own feelings and bitterness to inform their communications, communication suffers.

Some parents communicate as if they are the child's sole parent and subsequently fail to collaborate or engage with the other parent. As an example, one parent may schedule to take a child to a doctor's appointment without telling the other parent or even considering that the other parent should have been told about the appointment. Or a parent may purposely fail to give the other parent's contact information to a medical or psychological provider, resulting in one parent being essentially "left out in the cold" when it comes to the child's medical information.

A parent may fail to answer questions asked of them or intentionally or unintentionally delay the process of making decisions, both of which will be detrimental to the child. As an example, if one co-parent would like to register the child for summer school and asks the other parent about it, but the other parent fails to respond, the result is often that the child cannot attend because the program has filled up by the time the parents address the issue.

Parents may also communicate regularly, but ineffectively. Examples of this type of communication include a barrage of multiple emails in a short period of time, catastrophizing language (use of "always," "never"), bringing up the past, bad language, blaming, name-calling, criticizing, and bringing up topics not related to parenting.

To communicate effectively, co-parents need to come to some resolution of their differing communication styles, set up boundaries and rules for communication, and learn to conduct co-parenting communication in a businesslike manner, which includes the prompt exchange of information about the child.

B. Gatekeeping Issues

Co-parenting can't be discussed without discussing the concept of "gatekeeping," which means that one parent or the other is more in possession or control of information about the child or has more control of the child himself.[6] How that parent (the "gatekeeper") controls or manages the child's relationship with the other parent can be a big point of conflict between parents.

With intact relationships, gatekeeping is often intentionally practiced by the family. You may recall that your mother was always "in charge" of scheduling and attending doctor's appointments or that your father was the parent who always attended parent-teacher conferences. In this way, your parents were gatekeepers. The gatekeeping parent may be the one who knows all the child's teachers and medical providers, is responsible for all the phone calls to caretakers, and takes the children to all their appointments and activities. That gatekeeper parent may report to the other parent about what's going on (or the other parent may not need or want a report), and the parents may be perfectly happy with their unequal status when it comes to the children because the family is still together, and that arrangement works for the family.

Gatekeeping, when not restrictive, can be a typical and even valuable aspect of parenting. It is a form of specialization that couples arrange when they're together to best get things done. In the couples' relationship, one parent may have flexibility with their work schedule while the other is required to be at work for specific hours each week. Gatekeeping can be viewed on a continuum running from facilitative (helpful), cooperative (parents working together), disengaged (parents keeping away from each other), protective (one parent acting as a buffer or guard for the child), and ultimately to restrictive or very restrictive (one parent actively keeping the child away from the other parent).

Very
Facilitative → Cooperative → Disengaged → Protective → Restrictive → Very Restrictive

Gatekeeping can be justified or unjustified.[7] Gatekeeping is certainly justified when one parent has more time and flexibility to handle the child's schedule and transportation. It is when gatekeeping becomes restrictive, intended to actively and intentionally prevent the other parent from obtaining information and making decisions about the child, that gatekeeping becomes a problem and may require parent education or co-parenting counseling or, worst case, takes the parents to court to argue about the issue.

When parents separate, an unequal gatekeeping arrangement can suddenly feel harsh and unfair to the non-controlling parent. The gatekeeper parent may feel the status quo should be maintained for the benefit of the child, and they should remain in charge of all information. This tension in post-separation gatekeeping often leads to difficult co-parenting situations. Both the former gatekeeper and the former non-gatekeeper need to be aware of the changes they both must make because of their separation/divorce. Changing the nature of what was a long-standing parenting relationship is often very difficult and doesn't happen immediately.

After separation, when a parent intentionally withholds time and information about the child from the other parent, it is considered "restrictive gatekeeping," which is problematic when parents are trying to co-parent. Restrictive gatekeeping can be a pathway to a child's estrangement from one parent.[8] While gatekeeping is often a normal relationship that the parents created and agreed on during their relationship, restrictive gatekeeping after the parents separate is harmful to the child and to each parent's relationship with the child.

C. Exposing the Child to Parental Conflict

A child may be exposed to numerous forms of parental conflict. This may be directly expressed (e.g., yelling, threatening, bad-mouthing, or asking the child to spy on the other parent), or it may take the form of passive parental conflict (e.g., a parent's refusal to allow the child to have a picture of the other parent in their room, or a parent acting sad when the child speaks about the other parent). No matter how the child is involved in the parents' disputes, the child will suffer. Repeated studies have shown that the parents' relationship and interactions affect a child's well-being.[9]

"Triangulation" is a common form of conflict among separated or divorced co-parents. Triangulation occurs when two people in a family bring in a third party to soften the effect of the tension that exists between the parties and can include the parents bringing the child into their conflict, possibly to attempt to reduce a parent's stress level and to make the parent feel like they have an ally. Triangulation can be simply described as the child feeling "caught in the middle."[10]

Triangulation

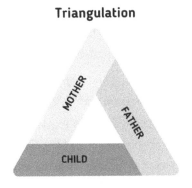

© 2024 Nicole Siqueiros-Stoutner

There are many reasons triangulation occurs. One example is a parent who tries to gain favor with or sympathy from the child. Other reasons are more complex, such as a parent wanting to use the child to influence the other parent's actions or feelings.

When children are triangulated into parental conflicts, one parent is trying to form an alliance with the child against the other parent. Often, in triangulation, the child is used as a communication channel or a pawn. By having an ally (the child) the parent feels that their position is stronger.

Here are some examples of triangulation:

- A parent asks the child to report back to them as to what the other parent is doing with their money or what's going on with their romantic life.

- Parent A tells the child to tell the other parent that the child wants to live with Parent A, knowing that may sway Parent B's feelings about custody arrangements.

- A parent tells the child negative things that were said by the other parent with the hope the child will believe it and dislike the other parent.

The situation is worse when the parents pass messages through the child (instead of speaking with each other), placing the child squarely in the middle of conflict. Parents may not always intentionally create triangulation; however, triangulation has been shown to result in adverse effects for the child.[11] These include self-blaming behaviors and diminished parental-child relationships.[12]

D. Parent-Child Contact Problems and "Alienation"

During a divorce or separation, children may reject contact with a parent. Parent-child contact problems (PCCP) can happen for many reasons, including child developmental factors, specific conduct by one or both parents, domestic violence, child abuse, age-appropriate affinities with one parent, similar interests or alignments with one parent, a parent's personality disorder, loyalty binds, maturity of the child, and other factors. Some of these factors lead to a justifiable rejection of a parent by the child; some rejections are not obviously justifiable.[13] No matter the causes, the outcome is often devastating for parent and child.

When a child is resisting time with one parent, the parents are often referred to as the "favored" and the "targeted" (or "rejected") parent.

This issue of contact problems may also be called parental alienation, alienation, resist-refuse dynamics, or other names, some of which lay blame for the issue on one parent based on specific conduct.[14] Harmful conduct is often denied by the rejected parent, leading to never-ending attempts to prove or disprove the conduct, rather than focusing on the child's interests and how the situation can be resolved. The favored parent may deny doing anything to influence the child's reaction to the rejected parent.

Not all high-conflict divorces or separations involve parent-child contact problems, but many do. Some children can navigate a high-conflict relationship between their parents without resisting contact with either parent. A family with several siblings may experience PCCP with one or two children, while the other siblings do not resist contact with a parent.

Contact problems between a parent and child are the subject of numerous books, research articles, online articles, blogs, and social media posts. The polarization of opinions about PCCP often pits fathers against mothers, with mothers alleging that the family court system doesn't adequately address domestic violence or child abuse issues, and fathers alleging that their parental rights are ignored by the system. Both positions have an element of truth, but the polarization usually makes the problem worse for the child.

When the issue is called parental alienation (PA), the blame for the rejection is placed on one parent—the favored parent. That dynamic has created one of the most controversial, debated, and misunderstood concepts in family court. In general PA happens when one parent deliberately attempts to coerce or convince a child not to have a relationship with the other parent, resulting in rejection of the other parent by the child. Alienation can be described as a systematic campaign by a parent to disrupt the relationship between a child and a parent.[15] It's important to recognize that PA is not always what led to PCCP.

PA is difficult to specifically define and recognize and generally happens on a continuum of very mild to very severe cases. In the mildest of alienating acts, a parent may redirect the child when they talk about the other parent, unintentionally allow the child to hear other family members speaking negatively about the other parent, or to allow the child to know too much about why the parents are not together. Severe alienating acts include direct statements to the child "We hate your father. He left us." "Your mother is an alcoholic and a horrible person and will never get a job."

The child's rejection itself happens on a continuum. In some cases, a child entirely rejects any contact with the parent, refuses to attend any parenting time, and becomes hostile when "forced" to engage in parenting time. The rejection may expand to include the targeted parent's extended family and home. In other cases, the child may agree to have parenting time with the rejected parent but will be rude and nonresponsive during the parenting time.

While PA is generally thought of as intentional or deliberate, a parent may also unintentionally alienate a child from the other parent through misunderstandings and lack of education about what should and should not be discussed with the child. In those cases, parent education can help the parent understand how their actions are affecting the child's relationship with the other parent.

Importantly, a child's rejection of a parent may or may not be due to alienating behaviors of the other parent. Unless specific alienating behaviors of the favored parent can be identified, it is more beneficial to focus on the problem (the child's resistance or refusal) rather than simply blame.

When a child resists or refuses contact with a parent, the underlying reasons must be explored, along with other factors, including:

- Previous relationship, if any, between the child and the targeted parent
- Favored parent's role in the child's actions
- Extent to which the targeted parent's actions have contributed to the child's resistance to that parent

Professionals working with divorced and separated families have studied allegations of parental alienation and parent-child contact problems for decades. Johnston and Kelly (2001) published a seminal article[16] on alienation dynamics that summarized several factors that may lead a child to reject a parent.

- Separation of family
- Aligned parent's personality
- Aligned parent's negative behaviors
- Conflict during marriage
- Siblings and sibling behaviors
- Child's adjustment, vulnerability, resilience, ability to cope, temperament, age, maturity
- Rejected parent's personality
- Rejected parent's negative behaviors
- Pressures of divorce litigation
- Alignment of family members
- Alignment of professionals

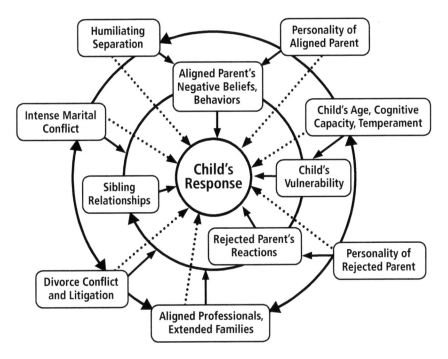

© 2001 Kelly, J.B., & Johnston, J.R.
https://www.apakazigazsagert.org/sites/default/files/alienated_child_art.pdf

While there are no easy answers about how to deal with PCCP, Chapter 14 discusses some potential interventions.

E. Personality Disorders and Mental Health Issues

No discussion of difficult co-parenting is complete without mentioning personality disorders and other mental health issues. These issues are covered extensively on the internet, and many divorced or separated people start discussions with their attorneys by saying, "He's a narcissist," "She has OCD," or "She has borderline personality disorder." The reality is the diagnosis may or may not be right. Casual diagnosing of people is not a good idea, as diagnoses occur only when someone has actually sought care and been seen by a licensed professional. When it comes to trying to co-parent with another, the diagnosis probably doesn't make any difference. The person with the personality disorder or mental health issue will still have a right to parent a child as long as they can parent safely.

Co-parenting with a person who has a personality disorder or mental health issues is decidedly difficult. A personality disorder, by definition, can affect a person's ability to appropriately make decisions, act in socially acceptable ways, communicate, and prioritize issues.

Mental illnesses often lead to perplexing behaviors and interactions that can be challenging for co-parents. People with personality disorders and other mental health issues may encourage conflict and have poor boundaries. Sometimes they don't know when to stop. Individuals affected by these conditions may have a difficult time communicating in an appropriate way and may act in ways that are inconsistent or unusual. They may struggle with prioritizing issues and focusing on the child's needs.

It can be helpful to consider your co-parent's mental health in interacting with them by concentrating on the traits you perceive to be counterproductive to co-parenting. Work to manage those behaviors rather than worrying about whether there's an actual diagnosis.

To be an effective co-parent, it is important to make strong, consistent efforts to set boundaries to keep things as stable as possible for the child. This book is full of ideas on how to do that. We also encourage parents to examine their own thoughts and actions to be sure they are maintaining their own boundaries and to ensure that they are not contributing to the conflict or prompting the other parent's behavior.

F. Substance Abuse of a Parent

When a parent abuses alcohol or drugs, research shows that their children have difficulty across all stages of development.[17] A parent's ability to co-parent is compromised when they misuse substances. Substance abuse can significantly impact co-parenting, causing heightened conflict and tension between parents and negatively affecting parenting skills and attachment. Parents may have struggled with substance abuse prior to the divorce or separation, and the separation may exacerbate substance use.

Erratic behavior, impulsivity, impaired decision-making, and frequent absences associated with substance abuse can create instability and uncertainty for the other parent and the child.[18] Substance abuse can strain communication and cooperation between co-parents as trust erodes and concerns about relapse and the potential negative impact on the child's life arise. Resolving these conflicts requires open communication, professional intervention, and a focus on the child.

When one or both parents are abusing substances, domestic violence may also be present. Substance abuse can lead to an increase in the level of domestic violence and conflict.

G. Domestic Violence

Domestic violence or "intimate partner violence" (DV/IPV) can be defined as a pattern of behavior in any relationship that is used to gain or maintain power and control over an intimate partner. It includes physical, sexual, emotional, economic, or psychological actions or threats of actions that influence another person.[19] The United States Justice Department's definition is similar, stated as "Domestic violence is a pattern of abusive behavior in any relationship that is used by one partner to gain or maintain power and control over another intimate partner. Domestic violence can be physical, sexual, emotional, economic, psychological, or technological actions or threats of actions or other patterns of coercive behavior that influence another person within an intimate partner relationship."[20]

While the discussion above reflects generally accepted broad definitions of domestic violence, it is often defined by statutes related to criminal or family cases. A particular jurisdiction (state or federal) may limit the definition of DV/IPV to certain specific acts. The discussion above reflects generally accepted broad definitions of domestic violence.

Engaging in DV/IPV is unquestionably ineffective co-parenting. The existence of DV/IPV in a parenting relationship requires attention to its effects on children, protection for the victim, and the use of parallel and disengaged parenting for the protection of all parties. Experts differ on whether parents with a domestic violence history can or should be required to co-parent or if co-parenting can be done effectively between perpetrator and victim. In the authors' personal opinion, when there exists a significant history of DV/IPV, co-parenting may be possible when there are strong boundaries between the parents and parallel parenting models are in place, as discussed in Chapter 3. Parents with DV/IPV backgrounds can also benefit from the use of a PC or mediator with a strong background of domestic violence training.

The safety of the child is the paramount concern when DV/IPV is present in a family relationship, followed by protection of the safety and well-being of the victim parent, respecting the right of the victim parent to direct his or her own life, holding perpetrators accountable for behavior, and allowing the child access to both parents.[21] Restrictive orders (such as supervised parenting time or supervised exchanges) and orders of protection (sometimes called protective orders or no-contact orders) are usually considered. At minimum, co-parenting needs to be arranged so that the parents do not have a lot of contact with each other. The parallel parenting concepts we talk about starting in Chapter 3 will help to disengage the parents.[22] Most importantly, recognition that DV/IPV exists in numerous forms and separating the various patterns of DV/IPV in a particular family is necessary before parenting arrangements or restrictions on parenting can be put into effect.[23]

H. How Ineffective Co-parenting Harms Children

Any of the forms of ineffective co-parenting discussed in this chapter, such as poor parent communication, exposing the child to parent's conflict, parent-child contact problems, mental health disorders, substance abuse, and domestic violence, can be devastating to children and may cause lifelong damage to a child's well-being.

Poor communication and high conflict between parents can be traumatic and extremely stressful for children. According to studies, this is one of the most significant factors for children and adolescents' behavior problems.[24] Parental conflict and protracted litigation (never-ending court battles) are linked to child problems, including delinquency, antisocial behavior, conduct problems, and academic issues, as well as emotional problems like insecurity, depression, and anxiety.[25] The negative impact of divorce may continue into a child's adulthood. Adverse effects include increased levels of substance abuse and mental disorders, poorer educational achievement, occupational and marital adjustment problems, difficulties forming healthy relationships, and overall reduced life satisfaction.[26]

Research shows triangulation is a significant risk factor for children caught in the middle of parental disputes. Children engaged in triangulation are at risk for emotional difficulty and excessive reactions to life's problems, particularly anxiety, depressive symptoms, and social withdrawal.[27]

Children are uniquely and negatively affected when a parent has a substance abuse disorder. The adverse consequences include the child having unmet developmental needs, impaired attachment, economic hardship, legal problems, emotional distress, and sometimes becoming the victim of violence. There is also an increased risk of the child developing a substance abuse disorder.[28]

The negative effects of domestic violence are extensive and well-documented.[29] Children who witness DV/IPV or are victims of abuse themselves are at serious risk for long-term physical and mental health problems. Young children who witness or are aware of violence in the home may revert to earlier stages of their development.[30] They may also be at a greater risk of being violent or being the victim of violence in their future relationships.[31]

Among various family stresses, parental conflict seems to have the most detrimental impact on children.[32] That is why there must be a solution for a child's well-being now and in the future.

CHAPTER 3

Parallel Parenting: Is It a Solution?

Parallel parenting is a form of co-parenting meant to reduce conflict and minimize harmful effects on the child. In parallel parenting, both parents (who are separated and/or divorced) assume or are assigned specific full responsibility for parental duties during their own time with the child. The parents minimize or even eliminate contact with each other in order to limit the child's exposure to the conflict and to limit the stress on them-selves.[33] "Minimize" as used here is just another word for disengagement.

A similar definition of parallel parenting is found in the writings of Philip Stahl, Ph.D., who wrote that it is "a style of parenting in which both parents learn to parent their child effectively, doing the best job each can do during the time the child is in their respective care. Parents disengage from each other so that conflicts are avoided."[34]

Dr. Stahl's paper recognizes that disengaging the parents through parallel parenting rather than engaged co-parenting leaves fewer opportunities for conflict between the parents, which benefits the child.

According to Dr. Stahl, the term parallel parenting probably came from the child development concept of parallel play, the period in child development when children (usually around age 18-36 months) play next to each other and might be aware of each other, but they don't really interact. Children's interactions come later, at ages 3-4, which is called associate play, and later, children move into cooperative play. If parents are good at parallel parenting for several years, they also might move on to cooperative co-parenting as well. The initial point of parallel parenting is to reduce conflict and allow each parent to be independent.

Parallel parenting is probably the most prevalent post-separation co-parenting arrangement for high-conflict families.[35] According to Dr. Matthew Sullivan, this is true because "conflict is dependent on interparental interaction." Thus, the lower the level of engagement between parents, as in parallel parenting, the lower the conflict level.[36]

Parallel Parenting Plans are appropriate for parents who:

- Don't get along well
- Are highly reactive to each other
- Have a history of family violence, including emotional and psychological violence
- Feel extremely uncomfortable or anxious in each other's presence
- Have an order of protection (restraining order) restricting contact
- Cannot cooperate in one or more major areas of parenting.

A. Key Concepts of Parallel Parenting

The key concepts in parallel parenting are (1) each parent is an autonomous and fit parent to the child, and (2) the parents don't have to deal with each other very much.

There is no need for two competent parents who have joint legal decision-making authority to talk to each other frequently unless they both want to. Giving up on being friends with your ex isn't giving up on your child. Parallel parenting is not a failure—it's a methodology.

Parents may be relieved to hear the findings of Joan Kelly's research that states children whose parents engage in low-conflict parallel parenting appear to thrive as long as they have adequate parenting in both homes and well-articulated parenting agreements.[37]

In parallel parenting, there is a recognition that reducing opportunities for conflict between parents is better for the child. It is well-established in research that children who are exposed to high conflict, arguments, and disputes between their parents are more likely to experience adverse results such as an inability to control and process anger, establish relationships, and learn their own dispute resolution skills. If the parents don't get along, feel uncomfortable in each other's presence, just prefer not to deal with each other, or if they have court orders in place that prohibit their contact with each other, then it's best for the child to have parents that develop and follow a Parenting Plan that eliminates their opportunities to interact and engage in conflict with each other.

The general framework of parallel parenting includes the following key concepts that set boundaries for the parents:

- The parents disengage with each other and have few or no interactions. Any communication they do have will be polite and businesslike.

- Each parent has been considered by the court to be "fit" to care for the child during their specific parenting time.

- Each parent accepts the other parent and their parenting style.

- A parenting schedule has been created that specifies times and dates, and each parent agrees to follow the Plan. Nothing is left open to interpretation.

- The parents avoid casual arrangements and stick to a fairly strict schedule. In order to minimize conflict, there is no assumption of flexibility in scheduling. Both parents follow the calendar. While flexibility sounds good in concept, being flexible leads to misunderstandings and disagreements. In a difficult case, any change to the regular schedule is an opportunity for misunderstandings and conflict. Changes to the Parenting Plan are not encouraged and are sought in only extraordinary circumstances.

- If any change from the regular parenting schedule is necessary, the parents will discuss and negotiate the change, sometimes with the help of a neutral person. This neutral person, such as a mediator or PC, may be necessary to resolve issues that aren't covered in the Plan. Discussion takes place using brief, business-like emails.

- For day-to-day parenting decisions, the parents work inde-pendently of each other. Each parent's household functions independently, and each parent is responsible for making deci-sions about the child during the time the child is in that parent's household. Neither parent tells the other parent how to parent, and neither parent criticizes the other parent's decisions.

- Meetings between the parents are public and formal, not private. Meetings are treated in a businesslike way and are scheduled by appointment at mutually convenient times. The parents may choose to have all meetings online or through email.

- Major decisions are made through exchange of information and identification of specific issues that need to be decided jointly. Ma-jor decisions generally include non-routine medical care and ap-pointments (specialists, specific conditions or diagnoses, and new medications that are recommended for the child). The parents do communicate in the event of emergencies involving the child.

- When parents need to share information with each other, they use email, a shared (online) calendar, or other written communi-cation. They should never use a child for communicating, and the parents avoid face-to-face communication whenever possible. Emails between the parents are businesslike and stick to specific issues about the child without name-calling or reference to past personal history or events. The parents avoid telephone conversations, as setting boundaries during phone calls is very difficult. Phone calls lead to miscommunication and he-said-she-said because so much emotion is involved. If the other parent insists on calling, voice mail can be used to disengage the communication. The person receiving the message can take time to listen, consider, and formulate a response, then reply with a succinct, brief, and businesslike email.

- Most transition times for the child take place at school, at a child-care center/program, or activities, meaning one parent drops off at the beginning of an activity, the other picks up at the end. This minimizes parents' conflict and in-person contact and makes the transitions easier for the child. It's usually easier for a child to go from the classroom to a parent's house rather than leave one parent's house to get in the car with the other parent. Exchanges at a parent's house should happen only when absolutely necessary, such as a holiday or a sick child.

- As much as possible, each parent takes responsibility for getting information about the child directly. Each parent is expected to obtain school information, calendars, and contact information for teachers and coaches directly from the source and not from the other parent. Each parent will have their own calendar to keep track of meetings, report cards, appointments, sports schedules, lessons, and the like. Neither parent is expected to remind the other about important activities that involve the child. While some of those important activities will be on the shared calendar (such as when report cards are due, when a field trip takes place, or when school pictures will be taken), others may not be on that shared calendar, and each parent is expected to keep the other informed about school communications.

B. Using a Parenting Coordinator Can Support Parallel Parenting

So far we've discussed both parallel parenting and, in Chapter 1, parenting coordination. What is the relationship between the two? Essentially, each facilitates the other. Parenting coordination is a hybrid of mental health and legal processes that provide hands-on, one-on-one parenting management, education, dispute resolution, and coordination of communication by a PC. Parenting coordination can be valuable for parents on the very conflictual side of the spectrum, but can also be useful, probably as a short-term solution, for parents who do not consider themselves to be high conflict but who need assistance in managing their co-parenting relationship. Parenting coordination is designed to be as available, or as circumspect, as an individual situation warrants.

Parenting coordination can help create and implement a parallel parenting arrangement by reviewing how the levels of engagement and conflict between parents have developed and expanded and how those levels can be mitigated through good communication and boundaries. A PC can help you develop and follow an effective co-parenting Parenting Plan based in parallel parenting.

C. Implementing Parallel Parenting Concepts in Your Plan

Joan Kelly's research[38] emphasized that children whose parents engage in conflict-free parallel parenting appear to thrive as long as they have adequate parenting in both homes and highly detailed parenting agreements and orders specifying contact and when joint decision-making is required. It's important to note that this positive outcome depends on a clear Parenting Plan designed to minimize conflict.

Co-parenting can be stymied by a deficient Parenting Plan. Sometimes the co-parenting problem is not so much about the parents as it is about the written Parenting Plan the parents are trying to follow. When this is the case, creating a Parenting Plan based on the principles of parallel parenting can be a solution.

General rules for a good, workable Parenting Plan that incorporates concepts of parallel parenting include:

- Specific days and times of day when each parent is responsible for the child.
- Specific days and times that school and childcare centers/providers are open as they may not always be open for a child exchange to happen there.

- Minimal communication between parents to figure out who has the child and when, and very little is left to last-minute negotiations.

- Using the word "reasonable" as little as possible because most parents simply can't always agree on what is reasonable.

- Using the word "flexible" as little as possible, for the same reason as above; flexibility isn't well-defined and means very different things to different people.

- Expectations for the autonomy of each parent. The Plan recognizes that the two parents' households will have different rules and values and judgments, both parents have the right to parent their child in the way each feel is best, and both households should be able to operate without influence and judgment from the other.

- Assumes and states that each parent will exercise good parental judgment when caring for the children without interference and input from the other parent.

- Covers most of the complaints and disagreements which are brought to a PC such as vacation scheduling, holidays, notice that should be given to the other parent, telephone calls, and travel.

- One that not only allows but *requires* each parent to be aware of the child's school work, activities, schedules, medical care, and other important information so that one parent is not the gatekeeper for all information.

Once the Plan document itself is in good working order, the parents can concentrate more on parallel parenting with each other to reduce conflict and stress on everyone (but particularly on the children).

In conclusion, here are four things you can do to get used to the idea of parallel parenting to avoid unintentionally doing things that might alienate your co-parent:

- Allow the child to love the other parent. Don't fall into the trap of criticizing the other parent. If you have difficulty allowing a child to express good things about the other parent, or allowing the child to love the other parent, that's a problem that needs to be addressed in personal therapy.

- Accept that you can't "fix" the other parent, and stop trying. If necessary, lower expectations for the other parent and for the co-parenting relationship. It's often the case that co-parents can't get to the point of being good friends who save each other a seat at the school concert.

- Accept that you can't force your parenting standards and styles on the other parent. Day-to-day decisions like bedtimes, nutrition, and discipline must be left to each individual parent.

- Practice empathy and understanding of your co-parent.

The co-parents' primary goal in parallel parenting is to reduce conflict, reduce contact between the parents, and maintain a businesslike, pleasant, and moderately distant relationship with the co-parent—not to tell each other how to parent.

CHAPTER 4

Communicating with Your Co-parent

Even if you aim to practice parallel parenting, as discussed in Chapter 3, you will still have to communicate with your co-parent to some extent, if only to create a Parenting Plan that requires as little communication as possible between the two of you. In this chapter, we'll offer some guidance on communicating effectively with your co-parent.

A. Using this Book with Your Co-parent

Let's start with some tips to help you approach your co-parent regarding using this book together. The following strategies may be helpful:

- Start by discussing your desire to find solutions to recurring co-parenting disputes and improving the co-parenting dynamic for the well-being of your child.

- Frame the discussion as a shared exploration of valuable insights gained from this book.

- Emphasize the common goal of creating a positive and stable environment for your child.

- Avoid blaming language or rehashing past conflicts. Instead, focus on the practical strategies, specific language, and solutions proposed in the book.

- Encourage the other parent to share their thoughts, concerns, and perspectives, which will hopefully foster a two-way dialogue.

It's important that you demonstrate your commitment to increasing co-parenting cooperation. Ideally, the other parent will demonstrate the same commitment. But, what if they don't?

John C. Maxwell said: "Life is a matter of choices, and every choice you make makes you." You have the ability to determine your own choices and actions. Your choices will undoubtedly influence your co-parent. However, you cannot control the other person's actions. In your co-parenting journey, there will be situations where the other parent will not be as committed as you are to bettering your co-parenting relationship and using some of the tools in this book. When that happens, you may have to take a deep breath and practice acceptance. That means you stop trying to influence or change your co-parent's behavior. Learning when to step back will reduce conflict and stress, allowing you to focus on what you can manage: your responses and the well-being of your child. Of course, sometimes stepping back isn't possible, such as when the well-being of your child is critically affected by what your co-parent is doing. In those moments, recognize that this particular issue does require you to address the concern with the other parent (hopefully as productively as possible). In analyzing your feelings and concerns about the issue and how best to approach the other party, look to trusted family, friends, and especially professionals for help and rely on their advice.

B. Less Blame, More Respect

The first rule of communication between parents may be the hardest.

Communication must show respect for the other person. A parent may find it difficult to respect the other parent based on past history and perceived wrongdoings. Despite the past, parents must show a basic level of respect for each other. Their dealings do not need to be overly friendly, but they must be businesslike and show basic courtesy.

Remember that inconvenient things are going to happen to kids, and not all those things are the fault of the other parent. Even intact families deal with smashed fingers, head lice, lost glasses, missing homework, and sick children. But when a child lives in two households, often these normal irritating things become ammunition against the other parent. *"He lost his glasses at your house AGAIN." "That stupid school you picked has given him head lice!" "She has this rash because of your neglect."* Before you blame a bad event on the other parent, stop to consider that things are often chaotic, and it's not necessarily the other parent's fault. Focus on fixing the problem and finding solutions rather than casting blame. Treat the other parent with a basic level of respect when discussing the problem and possible solutions.

"He lost his glasses – again. How can we get him a new pair as quickly as possible?"

Suggested response:

"What can we both do to make sure this doesn't keep happening? Here are a couple of suggestions..."

"He has head lice and the school sent home a letter about it. Here are the instructions: _____. Here is what I did: _____. I would appreciate you confirming that you received this information."

When a problem comes up, focus on dealing with the problem rather than blaming. There will be time later to figure out if something could have been avoided.

C. Choosing and Using the Right Communication

Parent communication might take place in person or by telephone, email, text, or by other online means. If parents have a history of being unable to communicate well, such as arguments, fights, loud voices, abusive language, physical altercations, and accusations, the parents should not plan on having in-person communication unless it's a true emergency. Telephone calls should also be avoided.

In the most difficult cases, the parents' communications about the child and parenting issues should be limited to email only. Email allows for asynchronous communication (meaning both parents don't have to be on email and writing at the same time). Each person plans when to review and respond to emails. Emails make a contemporaneous record of what was said and when. Using email wisely (as described in this book and others) can reduce conflict.

Parents often get caught up in texting each other. Texting should not be used for parenting issues for anything other than a very quick exchange of information, such as "I'm running 10 minutes late to our exchange." Texts too easily get out of hand and can lead to thoughtless and pointless fighting, especially with voice-to-text. High-conflict parents sometimes create texts that go on for pages and can become extended verbal fights on the screen.

Texting should not be used for important information. It's too easy to overlook a text with a medical appointment, date and time, or vacation plans, and important information can be missed or misunderstood. Texting may not keep a good record of information, and finding important information is difficult. Importantly, texts are difficult to print or forward to a third party, such as an attorney or PC, or for use in court.

You and your co-parent should be texting either very infrequently or not at all. If one parent persists in texting the other despite warnings not to, the other parent can move the conversation over to an email for the response. At least one parent (preferably both) should put down firm boundaries against texting to improve communication and move correspondence to email. Email allows the writer and the recipient to give more thought to the content and tone.

How emails are written between co-parents is very important. They should be businesslike and written as if they're written to a co-worker or supervisor. Court orders in high-conflict cases will often establish Email

Rules or Guidelines. Email Guidelines can also be set up by agreement, a PC, or custody evaluator. Here's a sample of some common Email Guidelines:

Email Instructions for Parents

Ignoring or failing to respond to emails from the other parent is not an option. Email communication is the preferred method for parents to communicate. These instructions should be followed for the most effective co-parenting communication.

SPECIFY AN EMAIL ADDRESS. One email address should be specified for use between the parents. You must check this email account at least once every day. Once an email is specified for this purpose, the other parent should not continue to send emails to a different email address.

BRIEF AND SPECIFIC EMAILS. Keep the email short. If you have more than one issue to cover, number the issues you are covering, and then the answering email should refer to each item by number. Above all, BE BRIEF and limit the emails to ONE OR TWO PER DAY unless there is a dire emergency.

FUTURE-ORIENTED ONLY. All emails relate to future activities, a request for future action, OR provide specific information. Emails do not re-hash past incidents. If you find yourself writing, "You've done this before" or "Remember when you . . ." it is a good sign that this writing is an email violation.

SUBJECT LINES. Use Specific Subject Lines on all emails. Ex: John's football practice; Melissa's dance; John's Dr. Appointment on January 30; John's football practice/dad's response on August 18". This is very important. The parents and the PC may end up with hundreds of emails in a file, and a specific subject line will help everyone locate the relevant emails quickly.

RESPECTFULNESS. NO name-calling, NO nick-names, and NO abusive language should be used. *All language should be respectful*. Write each email as if third parties are reading it (because they are).

COPIES TO PC. The PC (when one has been appointed) should be copied on all correspondence, including emails.

RESPONSES. Emails that require a response should be responded to within 48 hours of receipt. The same email rules apply to all response emails. When responding, do not bring up new issues in the same email. Answer the outstanding email/issue and start a new email for new issues.

NEW PARTNERS AND ATTORNEYS. New spouses (or significant others) obviously should not be involved in your co-parenting emails. They should not send emails about parenting, and they should not be copied on co-parenting emails. If you want to blind-copy your significant other with emails, or forward emails, you may do so, but the new spouse's name/email should not appear in the email itself. The same applies to your attorney. Do not copy them in the email, but you may forward emails to them later if you feel that's necessary.

FINANCIAL ISSUES. Do not talk about financial issues in emails that involve co-parenting or strictly child issues. Talk with your attorney about the best method for communicating regarding financial issues. Your attorney may suggest that emails not be used at all for financial issues (such as medical reimbursement requests) and instead be handled only by regular mail.

TEXT MESSAGING. Text messaging is not an approved form of communication for important or substantive things. Text messaging will not be used to give notice of anything important other than the fact that someone is running late or for an actual emergency to ensure that the other parent receives the message promptly.

Controlling email communication with the other parent takes knowledge, practice, and patience. Emails should not be written or sent in haste but should be carefully crafted using the guidelines below.

D. Keep It Brief, Informative, Friendly, and Firm

To make your emails with the other parent more effective and less stressful, we recommend using the BIFF Response® approach developed by Bill Eddy, LCSW, JD, of the High Conflict Institute. BIFF stands for:

- Brief
- Informative
- Friendly
- Firm

In general, BIFF responses (or "BIFFs") are written emails (or email replies), although BIFF works for in-person exchanges as well. The book *BIFF for Co-parent Communication* (2020) goes into detail about BIFF writing for co-parents. *No co-parent in a difficult or high-conflict situation should be without this book.*[39] Being brief, informative, friendly, and firm may seem easy and basic, but it can be difficult without a lot of practice. One key is timing. When you receive a difficult email full of accusations, misinterpretations, lies, and insults, you must step back and resist the urge to respond right away. A significant part of BIFF writing is considering your response before sending it.

Here's a short description of each aspect of a BIFF Response:

BRIEF: Your response should be very short, such as one paragraph of 2-5 sentences in most cases. It doesn't matter how long an email is that you're responding to; your response should be short. The point of this brevity is to avoid triggering defensiveness in the other person. Your response email is going to focus that person on problem-solving and future-oriented information.

To do this, don't give too many words for the other person to react to. The more you say, the more likely you are to trigger another long, conflict-laden response.

Keeping it brief isn't easy. The next step, keeping it informative will help you keep it brief. It is highly recommended that, whenever possible,

---

you give your proposed BIFF responses to someone else to review and edit before the email is sent. A reviewer who is familiar with the BIFF process will almost always shorten your response, and they won't be emotionally hooked.

INFORMATIVE: Give a sentence or two of straight, useful information on the subject being discussed. With a co-parent, this is usually straightforward information about an activity, doctor visit, a school issue, or passing on some information you've gotten from a third party. It may be a notification of the child's illness or notification of upcoming travel. If there is no real subject or issue (because the high-conflict communication you received is simply angry and venting), you can still give some related helpful information. Your response can shift the discussion to an objective subject rather than opinions about the other person's shortcomings. It's important to not include anything in the response that includes your opinion or any defensiveness about the subject. Just provide straight information presented in neutral terms, as briefly as possible.

FRIENDLY: Friendly is often the hardest part, but it's important. If you struggle with making it friendly, just replace 'friendly' with 'civil.' You can start with something like: "Thank you for telling me your opinion on this subject." Or: "I appreciate your concerns." Or just: "Thanks for your email. Here is some information . . .". You can also end your response with a friendly comment, no matter how hard that might seem. An example: "I hope you have a nice weekend."

FIRM: The goal for most of your BIFF responses to difficult emails from your co-parent is to end the conversation. This is definitely the case if you're trying to disengage from a potentially high-conflict situation initiated by the other parent. You want to let the other parent know that this is all you are going to say on the subject. You should stick to that resolution. In some cases, you will give two clear choices for future action, which would require an additional response from the co-parent.

If you need a response, then it will help to set a firm, reasonable reply date. If you are going to take action when the other parent does not do something, then you could say, for example: "If I don't receive the information I need by [reasonable date], then I will have to do [your action]. I would like your input." (Note that this is both firm and friendly.) Also note that, in general, asking for a response or input in a very short time is usually not reasonable, and your request for another response should give at least a few days unless that's simply not possible.

Remember the timing. Stopping to consider your response carefully and even doing several drafts of a response until you get it right are key. Even better, if you have someone relatively neutral and reasonable who can review your response before it's sent, get that helpful third-party input before finalizing and sending your response.

E. More Tips for Writing Effective Emails

In addition to making sure all elements of BIFF are present, consider these general rules about making emails more businesslike and effective.

Get to the Point Quickly

There's no need to have a lot of background, chit-chat, or small talk as part of a businesslike email. There should definitely be no apologies. (The BIFF book has an excellent section on why apologies are a mistake.) You can be friendly in an email and also brief.

[Original Email]

Joe,

I don't know why you keep asking me when Kevin's next teeth cleaning appointment is. I've told you like ten times. I'm good at making his appointments and I haven't forgotten.

That's a waste of three sentences for the writer to write and for Joe to read, and there's still no pertinent information in this email!

REVISED to be a BIFF response:

Joe:

Kevin's next teeth cleaning appointment is 8-15-21 at 3pm. Dr. Norton, as always.

Just get to the point. Don't take time out of your busy day to lecture, advise, or admonish the other parent. Getting to the point is BIFF's "BRIEF."

Use Bullet Points to Provide Succinct Answers

Where a longer email or response is needed on several parenting items, using numbered items or bullet points will keep the items organized. The use of bullet points and numbering will also be a reminder that parenting emails are businesslike.

Use of dense paragraphs of text encourages long, drawn-out narratives and explanations, and those narratives often turn into complaints or rehashing past events. Long narratives are also harder to read, and important items will be missed. Use bullet points often to summarize answers, solutions, and next action steps. Use bullet points or numbers in responses, even if the original email wasn't numbered.

If you find yourself writing a paragraph that's more than three sentences long, you're very possibly breaking the rules about rehashing past events or lecturing the other parent. An email full of long paragraphs is less likely to be read and understood. If something really is going to take up a lot of room, you should consider sending separate emails on separate issues.

Don't Speculate on Intent

It's hard to read emotions in emails, so don't try. You may assume that the other parent is doing something just because he's unreasonable, mean, or because he feels entitled. It really doesn't matter why the other parent wrote something. What is requested is either something you can agree to or not. Leave emotion out of your emails, both when writing your own emails and trying to interpret the other person's. Be logical and literal, and don't make assumptions. Don't say things sarcastically, as sarcasm doesn't come across well in emails.

Almost everything said to you by the other parent could be taken as blaming or negative. It's possible the other parent did mean to be negative towards you. So what? Figure out what the other person is trying to tell you or ask you. Can you agree to it or not? If you really can't figure out what they're saying or asking (because of negativity or emotions in the email), then your response email will ask for more information.

Determine What a Timely Response Is in the Situation

If your court orders or Email Guidelines give you a certain amount of time to respond to an email (24-48 hours are common time periods for response) then don't rush to respond to non-time-sensitive matters immediately upon receiving the email. If the other parent writes in April asking what your summer vacation plans with the children are, don't immediately fire back with a nasty email saying that it's only April, you have no idea, and you're not required to submit your dates until May. That response is not necessary or effective. Instead, sleep on the response that you will send to ensure that it is well thought-out and businesslike.

Pick Your Battles

One of the reasons to not immediately respond to the other parent's emails is to allow you to take time to pick your battles. The other parent's query about whether they can make a change to parenting time next week may incense you and make you want to write an accusatory email pointing out all the times they have changed things or refused to allow you to change times and how unreasonable they are. If you sleep on the question, you may decide that the swap of parenting time could actually benefit you. If you can make the requested change without much trouble, do it. This can be part of a larger strategy of picking your battles.

Answer Within a Reasonable Time Frame

Don't leave emails sent to you hanging for too long. Letting questions linger longer than a couple of days will create a backlog in your inbox and it will frustrate the sender. They will have to waste time tracking you down with follow-up emails. While you shouldn't feel obliged to answer every email immediately, and there may be good reasons not to, you should reply in a reasonable amount of time. Most Email Guidelines, including the guidelines in this book, call for a response to legitimate (reasonable) questions sometime within a set time period.

All parents are human, so there are exceptions to response times. A parent can't reasonably be a stickler for a 48-hour response rule if the question is sent at 5 pm on a Friday evening when the recipient is receiving the children and will have them all weekend. If the parent who has the children doesn't want to review and answer emails on Friday evening, Saturday, or Sunday during his custodial time, that's okay. Ideally, the parents can briefly check emails to see if anything is urgent or an emergency and can wait until the next business day to respond.

In general, co-parenting emails should be checked at least once every 24-48 hours, but not constantly. If you have a sick child or something specific going on, then for special circumstances you may want to be more frequent in checking and responding to emails.

If you can't reply with the answer within a couple of days, it's polite to respond by saying, "I received this and will get back to you by [specific date]." This is the way a business email would be handled, so that's how you should handle it with your co-parent.

Determine What You Really Need to Respond To

Here's a problem we often hear from a divorced or separated parent:

"They email me constantly! I have a barrage of emails, mostly about little things, several times every day and dozens of times a week. Most are too long to even read, and there's rarely any legitimate question about the children that needs to be answered. Do I need to read these emails? Do I need to respond when I can't figure out what they're talking about?"

Does this sound familiar? What should you do? What's a "legitimate" question in a parent email?

If a PC or other court official is overseeing your parent emails, that person can advise you. But if the court isn't involved and you don't have a PC, you will need to impose your own boundaries about what emails need to be responded to. It's possible you don't need to respond to some emails if they're not truly about a child-related issue.

One of the biggest mistakes separated parents make in their communications with a difficult ex is to try to respond to all their false and misleading remarks and allegations. It's human to think that you need to correct every misstatement with the belief that if you don't respond, it could be taken as an admission. People have a tendency to want to "correct the record" even when there isn't a record.

But continuing to respond to false and misleading remarks and allegations is a trap. When you respond to the false and inflammatory statements, the difficult ex sees you as engaged in the fight. They will not back off but will respond with more infuriating and manipulative statements to keep you engaged and riled up. When a parent is triggered and wants to "correct the record," the response is merely inviting more vitriol and will result in a series of emails that spiral into chaos.

When you receive inflammatory or manipulative emails, determine what you really need to respond to. Ignore the false, provocative, and inflammatory statements. Do not engage. Only reply to the specific issue that is actually important for the child.

If an email from your co-parent is focused on criticizing you as opposed to asking for information about your child, or the email is just not understandable, a response could be, *"I received your email. It's quite long, and I'm having trouble figuring out what you're asking. Could you very briefly point out any specific questions you have about [the schedule; the child], and I'll answer those questions as well as I can."*

A BIFF Response® can help you take control of emails. By not responding to the diatribe against you and returning to the issue at hand, you take control of the communication. A refusal to respond to the diatribe of nasty comments is not an acceptance of those comments. It's simply disregarding them to focus on the parenting issue. You, as the BIFF responder, are rising above to stay in the present and focusing on your child's needs. If the difficult ex continues to send off-topic rants, you can ignore them, or you can re-send your original response that was to the point.

Dealing with a difficult ex who communicates in this way is all about developing your own self-control and your own skills in responding. You alone control whether you will disengage from your co-parent's abusive behavior.

Use a Dedicated Email Address for Co-Parenting Communication

Be businesslike about where you do your emailing. You should have a separate, dedicated email address for co-parenting communication. If you use a work email address for communicating with your co-parent, you (a) run the risk that your emails are not private, and (b) run the risk of ruining your concentration and workday by combining work with co-parenting. By setting up a separate co-parenting email account (something like JasonsDad456@gmail.com), you can check that email periodically, but for the most part, you can set it aside during your workday. You open the JasonsDad456 email only when you're mindfully ready to deal with co-parenting issues. This kind of boundary-setting will allow you to concentrate on the Email Guidelines and will be better for your mental health.

F. Apps for Communication Between Parents

One benefit of the internet age is the availability of newer tools to improve upon older ones. In the last 20 years, a number of apps have been developed that offer real benefits and useful tools for parents to engage in productive post-separation communication and scheduling. The most popular is Our Family Wizard (OFW). At the time of publication, similar apps include Coparenter, 2Houses, Divvito, Fayr, 2ForKids, Amicable, AppClose, Talking Parents, Peaceful Parent, and CustodyXChange. These apps serve as automated parenting intermediaries at a low cost (OFW is $12.50 per month per parent as of September 2023 for the basic plan). While each app offers slightly different features, most include a shared calendar and communication (text and/or email) platform. (See Shared Calendars in Chapter 5.) Some of these apps include expense reimbursement tools, phone or video calling options, and access for third-party professionals. These apps offer sample orders to use in Parenting Plans on their website that address various features.

These apps promote boundaries by allowing you to save, compartmentalize, and isolate communications. They maintain all information for you, are easily searchable, and cannot be modified. However, most of these apps do not monitor content. The exception is Our Family Wizard, which has a Tone Meter AI function that provides immediate feedback regarding a parent's tone in communications sent on OFW. This feature is not foolproof, however, and it cannot monitor compliance with other rules like word count limitations.

If conflict is high between the parents, they may want to consider

ProperComm.com. This is an email and text web-based service that offers human monitoring of communications between high-conflict parties. This is particularly helpful in communications where a court has made a finding of domestic violence between the parents or has had to sanction a parent for inappropriate emails with the other parent.

A sample provision requiring the use of a communication app is as follows:

> The parents agree that each will sign up for and pay the required fees for the use of _____ [fill in name of co-parent app] to communicate regarding the child for a minimum period of ___ [fill in number of months or years]. Neither parent shall cancel or fail to renew their subscription. The parties shall activate and use the following features:
>
> [Address available features and how they will be used by the parties].

G. Don't Use the Child to Communicate

Do not use your child as a messenger of information (or a delivery person of physical items) between the parents' households. While this should be obvious, it still continues to happen. Do not give your child an envelope or package "to be delivered to Dad," even if the item is sealed and the child presumably doesn't know what's in it. Don't put a reimbursement check in the child's backpack. If there has been conflict between the parents, the child is aware of it. Your child doesn't know how the other parent will react to receiving something. Your child doesn't want to be questioned, "Do you have something for me from Dad?" Your child is not a messenger. Parents should use regular mail or a delivery service to get things between households unless they are items of a personal nature to your child. In that event, the child can help you pack their backpack to take to the other house, as long as they are transporting only their own belongings.

Also do not use the child to pass on messages. "Remind Dad that I'm picking you up early on Friday" or "Remind Mom that I'll be at the school meeting on Thursday" puts an unreasonable burden and anxiety on the child. These are communications that should be between parents, if the reminders are necessary at all. (If you're using a shared calendar, some of these "reminders" shouldn't be made at all, as they're on the calendar.) If something is important enough to communicate to the other parent, send a brief, specific email and don't ask the child to take on that responsibility.

For older children, if a parent is communicating directly with the child about the child's request for a change in schedule or the child's wish to do something once the child has requested something, do not say "Make sure that's all right with your mother." For one thing, the child might not tell you the truth. Many a parent has fallen for "Oh, Mom already said it's okay," only to find out later that Mom was never asked at all. After the child brings something up, a parent should respond "I'll check with your Mother about it" and then communicate directly between parents. A parent can later tell the child that the parents have talked and whether the child's request is acceptable or not. Ideally, the child should not know if only one parent turned down his request. The parents should be a united front.

Only when the child has firmly established that they are old enough and mature enough to handle communications between parents should the child be allowed to be the intermediary. While many 16- and 17-year-olds can do this, that responsibility is just too much for a 12- or 13-year-old.

Co-parenting can be tough, with challenges like different parenting styles, communication problems, and even lingering emotions from the breakup. The "golden rule" is to always put your child's needs first and be consistent in your actions. Remember that you have control over day-to-day parenting decisions while the child is with you but not while they're at the other parent's home. If you can do those things, your co-parenting journey will be less stressful and more positive, and your child will feel secure and supported.

PART 2

SAMPLE SOLUTIONS AND LANGUAGE FOR SPECIFIC SITUATIONS

In Part 2, we will discuss specific parenting situations where disputes may come up. For each situation, we suggest solutions to address and resolve concerns and conflicts, and we provide specific language that you can incorporate into your written Parenting Plan. In embracing these solutions, you and your co-parent can exist with less drama, which will reduce stress and trauma for you and, most importantly, for your child.

Most of the guidance in Part 2 applies to children school-age or older. Creating a good Parenting Plan for infants and toddlers is extremely difficult. If your child is very young, both you and your co-parent are encouraged to get as much education as possible about child development and infant/toddler needs in order to provide the child with everything they need. That said, we do offer suggestions for Parenting Plan provisions involving infants and toddlers.

CHAPTER 5

Timesharing/ Parenting Time

This chapter addresses the foundation of any Parenting Plan, such as, which parent the child is with at any given time. We'll address the basic schedule, how to track it and how to handle issues like sick days, holidays, and travel. By addressing these topics proactively and specifically in your Parenting Plan you can reduce opportunities for misunderstanding and conflict.

A. Residential Care: The Standard Parenting Schedule.

Whether it's called "physical custody," "physical residence," "parenting time," or the "regular schedule," there needs to be a basic timesharing schedule that spells out who the child actually lives with during specific time periods. The regular timesharing schedule forms the basis of the child's calendar, and it is overlaid by special days like holidays, vacations, and other specially defined days. Those special days and holidays are discussed later in this chapter.

The regular schedule can be made up of several different types of plans. Some of the most common regular schedules are:

Alternating Weeks Schedule

The child changes residences every week on a specific day (often Friday after school) and lives for a full week at a time in one parent's house.

Potential language: *The parents will have a relatively equal timesharing schedule of alternating weeks, with the child to change residences each Friday afternoon after school. If there is no school on a given Friday, the exchange time is 5 pm. The parent who is receiving the child is responsible for picking up the child either at school or the other parent's residence. If a child is ill during a school day, must be picked up from school early, or there is no school on a given day, the parent who has designated parenting time for that day is responsible for the child's care and transportation.*

5/2/2/5 Schedule

The child goes back and forth between homes more often than weekly. This plan is good when a child isn't old enough to be away from a parent for a full week. With a 5/2/2/5 schedule, the child is always with the same parent every Monday morning through Wednesday morning (return to school), then is with the other parent from Wednesday until Friday morning (return to school), then back with the first parent from Friday until the next Monday morning. This schedule ends up looking like this:

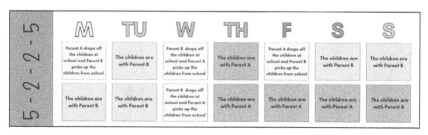

© 2024 Nicole Siqueiros-Stoutner

This calendar shows why the plan is called 5/2/2/5.

Potential language: *The parents will have a relatively equal timesharing schedule on a 5/2/2/5 schedule, with Mother as the Monday-Tuesday parent, Father as the Wednesday-Thursday parent, and the parents will alternate weekends from Friday school drop-off until Monday return to school, as follows:*

Monday 8 am to Wednesday 8am: Child with Mother

Wednesday 8 am to Friday 8am: Child with Father

Friday 8 am to Monday 8am: Alternating weekends.

2/2/3 Schedule

In a 2/2/3 schedule, the child goes back and forth every two days between households and then spends three days (the weekend, from Friday morning to Monday morning) in one household. The weekends are alternated. This plan is good for a child who potentially isn't mature enough for a 5/2/2/5 schedule and when neither parent wants to be away from the child for longer than a weekend (three days). This plan follows a repeating two-week schedule, which looks like this:

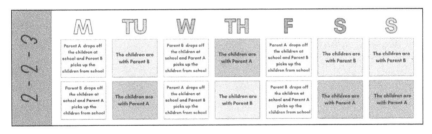

© 2024 Nicole Siqueiros-Stoutner

Potential language: *The parents will have a relatively equal timesharing schedule on a 2/2/3 schedule, with a two-week repeating schedule as follows:*

WEEK ONE Monday 8 am to Wednesday 8 am: Child with Mother

Wednesday 8 am to Friday 8 am: Child with Father

Friday 8 am to Monday 8 am: Child with Mother

WEEK TWO Monday 8 am to Wednesday 8 am: Child with Father

Wednesday 8 am to Friday 8 am: Child with Mother

Friday 8 am to Monday 8 am: Child with Father

Whichever parent had the child Monday-Wednesday in a given week will have the child for that following weekend.

On any day the child has school, the exchange time is drop-off at school. The parent with whom the child spent the previous overnight is responsible for taking the child to school the following morning.

If a child is ill during a school day, must be picked up from school early, or there is no school on a given day, the parent who has designated parenting time for that day is responsible for the child's care and transportation.

One issue with this 2/2/3 schedule is that a parent must be prepared to have the child on Monday/Tuesday during some weeks and on Wednesday/Thursday the following week, which requires more advance planning than having the child for the same weekdays every week. Any lessons, activities, or extracurriculars that the child is involved in must be carefully planned, as both parents will be very involved in transporting the child in this schedule. An advantage of this plan is that both parents will be very involved in activities that occur weekly.

Some Parenting Plans, unfortunately, aren't very specific and leave out who is responsible at given times. A Plan may state that Mother's parenting time runs from after school Monday until return to school Wednesday, and Father's parenting time runs from after school Wednesday until return to school Friday. Who then is responsible for the child during the school day on Monday and Wednesday? It's not clear. These are the kind of drafting errors in Parenting Plans that leave parents in high conflict and each blaming the other for something that really isn't their fault. That confusion is why the proposed language stated earlier uses specific exchange times of day, such as 8 am and 5 pm, to make it clear when each parent's parenting time starts.

The schedules listed above are all relatively equal parenting time schedules. (See Equal Time? In Section D.) While relatively (but not *exactly*) equal parenting time is very common,[40] there are certainly other parenting schedules where one parent has the child more during the school week. Those schedules can include language such as:

Mother will have parenting time with the child every Wednesday from after school (12 noon on non-school days) until return to school on Thursday morning (8 am on non-school days), and will also have the child on alternating weekends from Friday after school (5 pm if no school) until Monday return to school (8 am if no school). The child will be in the care of Father at all other times.

B. Infant and Toddler Parenting Time Schedules

It cannot be too strongly emphasized that when preparing a parenting time schedule for infants and toddlers, a mental health professional should be consulted to discuss the child's emotional and developmental needs.

Most importantly, parents must communicate more and frequently when a very young child is involved as schedules (feeding, bathing, sleeping) should be maintained in both households and children's needs are changing regularly. When a baby takes a regular nap every three hours or has a feeding every three hours, a failure to ensure uniformity of these schedules between homes may cause significant problems for the parents and the child. Consistency is key with infants!

New parents and caregivers may benefit from classes on child and baby first aid, child development, and infant and newborn care. These classes are available both in-person and online, at hospitals and other child welfare organizations. Attending these classes is useful, even for those with prior childcare experience, as they provide the latest information and tools. For instance, CPR guidelines for children have changed significantly since the 1990s. These classes will also impress on both parents an understanding of child development and the importance of the child's schedule. With that information in hand, ideally parents will be able to better communicate and work together when it comes to planning for the child and meeting the child's needs at their separate homes.

Only a few states in the U.S., such as Michigan, have laws requiring the courts to consider whether a child is breastfeeding[41] when determining parenting time. While the laws on this and most issues vary across jurisdictions in all countries, even without a specific law, the court may consider breastfeeding and related issues in parenting time determinations.

Regardless of a legal obligation to consider breastfeeding, there are challenges when crafting an appropriate Plan for a child who is breastfeeding. Primarily, parents need to address when and how the child will be fed when not able to breastfeed. Simply because one parent is able to express milk and one is not, does not necessarily mean the breastfeeding parent should have more time with the child. One parent can express milk and allow that milk to travel with the child during the other parent's time with the child. Families may want to begin allowing the non-breastfeeding parent's time to gradually increase so the child can adjust to bottle feeding breastmilk, and the breastfeeding parent's milk production/pumping schedule can also adjust. An example breastfeeding clause could be:

> *For a period of two weeks, Parent A's parenting time will begin at 11:30 am to allow Parent A to feed the child for his 12:00 pm feeding. Parent A's time will end at 2:30 pm before the child's next feeding. Thereafter, Parent A's parenting time shall be increased to 8:00 am until 4:00 pm every other day for a period of 14 days. During this time, Parent A shall utilize breastmilk and ensure the child continues to follow the agreed upon nap and feeding schedule with feedings at 9:00 am, 12:00 pm, and 3:00 pm.*

Infants and newborns benefit from frequent interactions with both parents, particularly during the child's waking hours. Both parents should engage in play, diapering, and feeding with the child to develop and enhance their parent-child bond. If one parent is less bonded with the child as compared to the other, that parent should begin with short and frequent bursts of parenting time and build up to more parenting time. Parents should focus less on equal time and more on ensuring they have regular quality time with the child.

If we assume one parent (Parent A) has been breastfeeding and providing primary care for the child and the parents are able to communicate and cooperate well enough to keep the child's schedule fairly consistent, the following gradually increasing infant schedule (or something similar) may work:

> *Starting on May 1st, Parent B shall begin with every other day for*

three to four hours beginning ____ and ending ____ [times selected during the hours the child is typically awake]. After a period of 30 days, Parent B's time shall be increased to 8 hours every other day beginning ____ and ending _____ [this should include times when the child is both awake or napping]. Parent B shall ensure that they have the appropriate supplies to transport, feed, diaper, and care for the child during their parenting time. Both parents agree to follow recommendations of the pediatrician as it relates to the child's schedule.

C. Should the Child Be Interviewed?

In most states, the child's wishes are one factor to be considered when the court has to make a decision about the parenting schedule. Even if the child's wishes are not a specifically stated factor, many parents want their child's wishes heard and some parents report that the child is demanding to be heard on the issue of where they will live and the overall schedule. How should the child's wishes be communicated? If they write a letter or are recorded (video or audio) for a statement, the other parent may be suspicious that the child is simply reciting what the parent wants them to say. A child should not, as a rule, be recorded (video or audio), particularly for use in court proceedings or to prove the child's wishes on an issue.

Child interviews are often conducted by an individual working within the court system or by a mental health professional. In smaller counties and jurisdictions, judges may even interview children, usually in chambers (private office) and not in open court. Interviewing a child is a highly specialized process and should be done only by professionals who have extensive training in child interviews so that the interview doesn't result in the interviewer leading the child, telling the child what to say, or causing the child to feel they are choosing one parent over the other. Skilled child interviewers will ask only open-ended questions that do not presume the answer and will find out information about all aspects of the child's life (interests, friends, schoolwork, pets, sports, etc.) and not just ask, "Who do you want to live with?" The child will be permitted to ask questions of the interviewer in order to feel safe about the process. The interviewer will try to find out if anyone has told the child what to say and if the child understands why they're talking to the interviewer.

Ideally, in order to find out a child's wishes or preferences this would be done in one interview and not repeated. If a child is interviewed or asked to make a statement by a parent or other non-professional person, more harm than good will result and a possible result is that the child's true wishes can never be ascertained.

D. Equal Time?

The question of whether the parents will have equal parenting time (also called 50-50 time) is beyond the scope of this book and is the subject of intense debate and research. Many parents will request equal parenting time when they separate even if childcare responsibilities were left mostly to one parent when the parents were together. If the question of equal parenting time exists in a case, both parents are encouraged to speak with their lawyers and experienced family law mediators to mediate a final Parenting Plan.

Attempts to have parenting time come out exactly equal usually reflect a parent's insistence on equality rather than what's truly best for the child. Most research studies refer to "shared parenting" as both parents having at least 35% of the child's time, which is far more likely to reflect reality than an attempt to divide time exactly equally.[42] Especially considering holidays and other special days, it is almost impossible for the division of parenting time to come out exactly equal in a given year.

The question of whether an equal parenting time schedule is appropriate for infants and toddlers is highly controversial. Infants and toddlers obviously have particular needs as well as an inability to express those needs (in words anyway). If Parenting Plans attempt to equalize parenting time for very young children, which results in the child sleeping in different homes every few nights (or even every other night), the child could develop behavioral and attachment issues that will show up as sleeping issues, lack of toilet training or other toilet issues, as well as behavioral and emotional issues.[43]

E. Using an Online Calendar

No matter what parenting schedule is agreed upon or ordered by the court, you will be wise to create an online shared calendar to show the schedule and to overlay the holiday and vacation schedule. Google Calendar is probably the best-known free app that can be shared between parents. Several online paid services offer shared calendars, including those mentioned in Chapter 4, "Communicating with Your Co-parent": Our Family Wizard (OFW), Coparenter, 2Houses, Divvito, Fayr, 2ForKids, Amicable.io, AppClose, Talking Parents, and CustodyXChange.

We suggest in several areas of this book that the parents try to use a shared calendar. This is suggested even where the parents are practicing strict parallel parenting and limiting their interactions with each other. In practice, the shared calendar will make it easier for the two of you to limit your interactions with each other. A shared Google Calendar is free. One parent sets up the Google Calendar and shares it with the other by email, after which both parents may insert calendar events and notes into the calendar. When vacations are scheduled, all itinerary information (flight numbers, times, locations, and addresses) is filled into the calendar for the specific dates. This reduces the need for emails between the parents.

One issue with a shared Google Calendar is that either parent can modify (or delete) entries made by the other parent, and (at least currently) Google doesn't track who made changes and when. If one parent modifying entries is an issue, the parents should review Our Family Wizard. That app (which has an annual fee) includes a shared calendar, but each and every entry is monitored and shows when each entry is made or modified and by whom. Parent A is not permitted to modify or delete entries made by Parent B. If Parent A claims that a certain calendar item was entered at a certain date, that can be verified, so late or modified calendar events can be spotted.

If considering using Google Calendar, familiarize yourself with its functions and its downfalls. Always make yourself aware of privacy settings and the appropriate way to share only the calendar (not email or other Google apps) with another Google user.

F. Working Parents and Childcare Considerations

While parenting schedules should be designed for the child's best interests, parents need to recognize that their own interests, availability, and
work schedules must be considered. It does little good to assign parenting time to a parent when they have to be at work and childcare will
be necessary for much of that time. If both parents profess to make a
determined effort to be available for the child during the school week, it
may work to divide the school week relatively equally. In that case, each
parent will be expected to act responsibly in seeing that the child completes and turns in all assignments, does all school projects and reading,
and studies for tests equally in each household. Working parents must
recognize that a child is likely to need third-party care providers at times.

G. Childcare and Caretakers

A parent doesn't lose parenting time just because one of them needs
childcare some of the time. Many children spend a part of each day in
childcare, whether it's before- or after-school care at the school or a private caretaker in the home. When parenting time is assigned to a parent, that parent is expected to provide appropriate childcare, as needed,
during their own time. That childcare decision belongs to the parent who
is assigned parenting time and is usually not subject to approval or over-
sight from the other parent.

Ideally, for infants and very young children, the parents can agree on
a single childcare provider or service that will be used when the child is at
either parent's home. Consistency in child care can give the child stability
and allow both parents access to the same day-to-day information about
the child.

H. When the Child Is Sick

The Plan should be specific about which parent has primary responsibility for staying home with a sick child on a school day, or picking up
a sick child when the school calls. If the Plan defines parenting time as
"Mother, from 8 am on Monday to 8 am Wednesday, and Father from 8

am on Wednesday to 8 am on Friday," then if a child is sick on Wednesday, Father would presumptively be the person responsible for their care or pick-up from school. This creates a situation where, if Mother notices that the child isn't feeling well or has a fever on Tuesday evening, Father should be notified right away so he can start to make plans to have a sick child on Wednesday.

The parenting time schedules mentioned earlier include a specific clause covering the sick child situation: *"If a child is ill during a school day, must be picked up from school early, or there is no school on a given day, the parent who has designated parenting time for that day is responsible for the child's care and transportation."*

The parents can agree to switch responsibility for a sick child. Obviously if the school calls about a sick child and the "primary" parent cannot be reached, the other parent should respond as quickly as possible. In most cases, the school will not know which parent has responsibility on a given day (the school isn't responsible for reading your Parenting Plan), so if the school calls the wrong parent, that parent should try to get in touch with the responsible parent. In the example above, if Mother received the call about the sick child on Wednesday, which is defined as Father's Day, it would be wrong for Mother to simply go to school and pick up the sick child without first trying to notify Father.

I. Holidays, Vacations, Special Days

Holidays, special days, and school breaks are those occasions that override regular parenting time. When a holiday, special day, or school break is specifically assigned to one parent in the Plan, that assignment overrides the regular parenting schedule. Think of the regular parenting schedule as the basic calendar, and holidays and special days are overlays—those schedules are entered in over the top of the regular parenting time and will have priority over regular parenting time.

The hierarchy of parenting time versus holiday, break, and vacation time is this:

Hierarchy of
parenting time

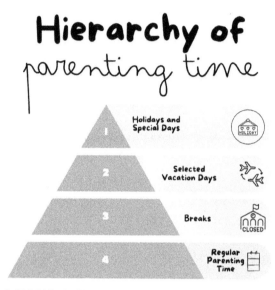

Holidays and Special Days
Selected Vacation Days
Breaks
Regular Parenting Time

If "special days" such as family birthdays conflict with holiday time, holiday time takes priority. As stated below in more detail, sometimes it's simply best to have all family birthdays (children's and parents included) follow the regular parenting time schedule, as birthdays will so often conflict with a holiday or a school break.

Parents should consider what holidays and special days are truly important to the family. No family should feel obligated to have cultural, religious, or national holidays treated specially on their family calendar if they are not really special days. Just because a certain calendar day is called a federal, state, or religious holiday does not mean it's treated as a holiday in a particular family's Plan. If a family has never celebrated Easter, it's possible that Easter Sunday and weekend should not be a specifically spelled-out holiday and that day and weekend should follow the regular parenting time schedule. If a holiday, special day, or day off school is not specifically mentioned and allocated in a Plan, that day follows the regular parenting schedule.

"Special days" also refers to events like a child's birthday (maybe even a parent's birthday) that overrides the regular parenting schedule. "Holiday" refers generally to holidays that are celebrated on a school calendar but also may include days such as Mother's Day, Father's Day, or days like Halloween when the child could be in school. The only holidays that apply to a specific family are those listed in that family's Plan. If other federal holidays are not listed in a family's Plan, then those federal holidays follow the regular parenting schedule.

Note that the fewer the designated holidays and special days, the more the regular parenting time calendar remains in place, which reduces conflict and misunderstandings between parents. It is highly suggested that the parents carefully consider what holidays are really important and limit the number of holidays and special days that change the regular parenting schedule.

Beware of including generalized "special days" that would change the parenting schedule. Some Plans have language like *"The parents agree to be flexible in allowing the children to attend other special days such as family weddings, funerals, reunions, and parties."* While that language sounds nice, it has led to innumerable disputes between parents. There is no specificity as to what someone considers a "special" event or to what extent the wedding or funeral of a distant relative would be able to override the regular parenting schedule. If the proposed special event happens to fall on a holiday that is already mentioned in the Plan, a dispute may arise about which takes precedence. Parents may also disagree about whether a child is mature enough to attend a family funeral or travel a long distance for the event. Parents who get along well can always discuss these special family events when they arise, but parents who do not communicate well about schedule changes find that this very vague provision causes problems and isn't really enforceable anyway. In general, any provision that relies on the words "flexible" or "reasonable" is ripe for dispute.

We discuss individual holiday and break periods below and at the end of this section, and how they can best be handled in a Plan, including some sample Holiday Schedules that you may want to consider for your own Plan.

Thanksgiving

Parents need to review their school calendar, which is in effect (or school calendars for schools in their general area), to see how a school district defines Thanksgiving, a holiday that always falls on a Thursday (if you're in another country, substitute a holiday that might be similar). There is a wide variety in the definition of Thanksgiving by different schools. A child may be off school the entire week of Thanksgiving, or may attend only Monday and Tuesday, or may attend Monday through Wednesday. Tuesday or Wednesday of that week may have early release. Some districts may make Thanksgiving week the same as fall break, so if a Plan allocates both fall break and Thanksgiving to different parents, there is a direct conflict in the Plan. If that occurs, it is suggested that the allocation of the holiday, rather than the break, takes precedence.

Halloween

While Halloween is a special day for most younger children in the United States and in some other parts of the world, consider having a termination clause for Halloween (meaning it is no longer considered a holiday) once the youngest child turns 12 or 13. After that time, Halloween would simply follow the regular parenting schedule. When children are younger, Halloween is often defined as after school until the following morning (return to school or 9 am) if it falls on a school day; if it falls on a weekend, Halloween can be defined as starting sometime in the mid-afternoon and running until the following morning. When Halloween is alternated by year, each parent will have the chance to spend Halloween afternoon and evening at parties or activities, and the child is not exchanged that evening. Instead, the child will have a good night's sleep at the home of the parent who was assigned the holiday that year.

Child's Birthday

The parents should consider whether the child's birthday should be considered a "special day" that changes regular parenting time. If the parents exercise substantially equal parenting time, each parent will have time with the child very close to the birthday and will be able to celebrate with the child either the weekend before or the weekend after the birthday. Maintaining the child's birthday as regular parenting time will simplify scheduling and reduce the opportunity for conflict between the parents. If a child's birthday must be included as a special day outside of the regular parenting schedule, specific times must be designated for the child's exchange.

The parents should consider how an exchange on the actual birthday will feel to a child. It is strongly recommended that the child not be forced to transition between homes on the actual birthday. Also consider if the child's birthday falls on or near other specially defined days such as Thanksgiving, Christmas, Boxing Day, Hanukkah, Father's or Mother's Day, or in the middle of summer where the birthday could conflict with summer vacation scheduling. If it does, the parents should discuss ahead of time how they will handle direct conflicts between, say, the child's birthday and Father's Day.

Parents' Birthdays

The parents should consider whether each wants their birthdays to be considered special days that change the regular parenting schedule. Including the parents' birthdays as special days could be problematic. If the parents absolutely feel their birthdays must be designated as special days so that the birthday parent gets the child that day, then specific times for celebration of the parent's birthday should be stated. The day of birth should be stated in the Plan so that anyone reading the Plan knows when it falls. If the parents' birthdays are likely to conflict or overlap with a school break or a specified holiday, perhaps the parents' birthdays should not be considered special days and should follow the regular schedule. This will greatly simplify scheduling and each parent will be free to celebrate the parent's birthday during regular parenting time closest to the birthday.

Overlap of Holidays and Special Days

When setting up a holiday schedule and awarding time to each parent, the parents must note where holidays, vacations, breaks, and special days overlap. It could be that a child's birthday will fall during a break period or holiday. If a child or parent has a summer birthday that is designated as a special day awarded to one parent, that birthday will have an effect on when each parent can schedule summer vacation. A child or parent's birthday may sometimes fall on the same day as Easter, Mother's Day, or Father's Day, or during spring break, and if that happens, there will be a direct conflict in the Plan. It is strongly suggested that if either a child or a parent has a birthday with an obvious conflict with a major holiday, then the Plan should specify that the birthday takes precedence *only if* it does not fall on the holiday or within the break period. If a child or a parent has a birthday falling during the summer, the Plan should specify whether that birthday has primary importance over summer vacation scheduling or whether a parent can schedule vacation over that birthday, if necessary.

Also beware of the potential overlap of Easter and spring break. If one parent is assigned spring break, that parent should also have Easter in the same year (even or odd-numbered year) in case the two periods overlap.

Cultural or Ethnic Holidays, Religious Holidays, or National Holidays.

Many families celebrate holidays that may not be considered typical American holidays. These holidays may be rooted in cultural traditions such as Diwali in India. They may hold religious significance such as Eid al-Fitr in Islam or Passover in Judaism. These holidays may hold a special significance to certain groups such as Juneteenth in the United States, an African American cultural holiday and a federal holiday that commemorates the end of slavery.

Families that value and celebrate cultural, ethnic, religious, or national holidays should consider them in their Plan. Ideally, when these holidays are added to a Parenting Plan the parents will address in their Plan how to handle traditions and customs related to the holiday, such as fasting on Yom Kippur or Ramadan, the children's attendance at prayer services or celebrations, and whether the children will attend school when they are observing these holidays. These sorts of discussions will reduce conflict.

Parents should be mindful that it may not be possible to account for every holiday they celebrated as an intact family. As an example, in Judaism, there are weekly Shabbat observances, other minor observances and fast days in addition to at least eleven annual significant Jewish holidays, including Rosh Hashanah, Yom Kippur, Sukkot, Hanukkah, Purim, Passover, Shavuot, Tisha B'Av, Tu B'Shvah, Lag BaOmer, and Simchat Torah. Jewish families may be comfortable agreeing to celebrate all of these holidays. Or, they may wish to agree that only the Jewish High Holy days (Yom Kippur and Rosh Hashanah) will be a part of their Parenting Plan, given how many holidays there are and the length of the holidays.

More importantly, parents need to clearly define the holidays in their Plan and include times, if appropriate. This is especially true for holidays that change on an annual basis. As an example, the South Korean holiday of Chuseok varies from year to year. In a simple online search, one will find at least two different start days for this holiday each year simply because it is based on the lunar calendar. In this situation, the best approach is to either select one source, such as a certain website or person who will define the holiday each year for the parties and notate that source in the Plan. Or the party who will be exercising this holiday to select the exact days of observance and provide advance notification to the other party of the days they will be exercising the holiday.

Some holidays may be observed over multiple days. This can also prove difficult to define and may cause conflict as there is the potential for major changes to a family's regular parenting time schedule. For instance, in Judaism, Passover is an eight-day holiday, and Sukkot may be celebrated for seven to eight days. In situations where a holiday spans more than a few days, parties should consider defining specific days they plan to celebrate that holiday. Another example: parents may define Ramadan for purposes of their Parenting Plan as the last three days of the sometimes thirty-day period because often these last three days will include a celebration known as Eid al-Fitr. The parties would then alternate only those three days in their Parenting Plan and follow their regular parenting time schedule for the rest of the Ramadan period.

Three-Day Weekends.

Generally, there are four three-day weekend periods that are recognized as federal holidays in the U.S. and that may occur during the school year:

- Martin Luther King Day, which creates a 3-day weekend in January
- Presidents Day, which creates a 3-day weekend in February
- Memorial Day, which creates a 3-day weekend in May
- Labor Day, which creates a 3-day weekend in September.

These are all Monday holidays, but in some states in the U.S., a three-day holiday may be created by a Friday holiday. Individual states also have their own special days off, which might be considered special days to mention in the Parenting Plan. California has Cesar Chavez Day (March 31), Massachusetts has Patriots Day (the third Monday in April), and Chicago celebrates Pulaski Day on March 7 (and schools are usually closed). In creating a Plan, the parents need to agree *either* that these days follow the regular parenting time schedule and that each parent recognizes they will need to provide childcare on those non-school days, *or* they need to specify exactly what the schedule is on those days.

Spring Break and Fall Break

These breaks are fairly standard days that school is not in session and are typically allocated between parents in a Plan.

Knowing the child's school calendar is crucial for a discussion on how to divide these breaks. Not every school district has both spring and fall breaks. These breaks generally should be alternated in the event no fall break occurs in a given year, that parent will at least have an upcoming spring break with the child. Note that if both breaks are on the school calendar, one parent will either end up with both spring break and fall break in the same calendar year (different school years) or a parent will have spring break in one year (i.e., odd-numbered years) and then won't have fall break until the end of the following year (i.e. even-numbered years).

Some districts may make Thanksgiving week the same thing as fall break, so if a Plan allocates both fall break and Thanksgiving to different parents, there is a direct conflict in the Plan. If that occurs, it is suggested that the allocation of the holiday rather than the break take precedence.

Defining spring and fall breaks. A Plan should specify when each break starts. Does it start at the end of the school day on the last day before break and end when school resumes? Or are these breaks defined only as the actual days off of school (Monday through Friday)? When those weekdays are combined with a parent's regular weekend parenting time, it creates a break period of a full week (Friday to Friday or Monday to Monday), which keeps the regular weekend schedule in place and causes fewer problems.

Winter Break/Christmas

A common division of winter break is that the entire break is divided in half, with an exchange on the midpoint day. A specific time for the exchange on the midpoint day and a method of calculating that midpoint day should be included in the Plan. Many winter breaks will start after school on a Friday and end on the Monday morning two weeks later. This results in winter breaks that are 17 nights long, an odd number, so a Plan should designate whether the first-half or the second-half parent gets the extra overnight. By defining that, the midpoint exchange day is defined.

A Plan may also "carve out" Christmas Eve and Christmas Day from the calculation, assigning one of those to each parent, which leaves 15 overnights in the winter break to be divided evenly. Common Plan language for this includes:

The child's winter break from school is divided equally. Break begins when the child is released from school on the last day before the break and ends when the child returns to school after the break. Mother has the first half of break in even-numbered years and Father has the first half of break in odd-numbered years. The child will be exchanged at noon on the midpoint day during the break. Regardless of which parent has the first half of the break, Christmas Eve is defined as commencing on December 24 at 8 am and runs until December 25 at 8 am. Father is awarded Christmas Eve in even-numbered years and Mother in odd-numbered years. Christmas Day is defined as commencing at 8 am on December 25 and runs until 8 am on December 26. Father is awarded Christmas Day in odd-numbered years and Mother in even-numbered years.

Here's an example of how that works to divide winter break and the Christmas holidays. This example assumes that winter break starts on Friday, December 17, and ends on Monday, January 3, where December 17 falls in an even-numbered year:

- Dec 12-17 to Dec 24 at 8 am   Child with Mother
- Dec 24 8am to Dec 25 at 8 am   Child with Father

- Dec 25 8 am to Dec 27 at 8 am   Child with Mother

In this example, December 27 is the midpoint day.

- Monday, Dec 27 to Monday, Jan 3 (school starts)   Child with Father

In this example, the child had nine overnights with Mother (the first half parent) and eight overnights with Father. That situation will reverse in the next winter break.

Times for exchanges are ideally specified for all holidays, but if a Plan doesn't have specifics and simply states "Christmas morning," the parents need to agree in writing to an exchange time, as there is no universal definition of what "Christmas morning" means. (See Travel During Winter Break in the travel section.)

Note: If the Plan's regular parenting time is an alternating week schedule, the parents may want to consider leaving winter break on the regular parenting schedule, carving out only special time for Christmas Eve and Day to make sure each parent has some time on those days. Under an alternating week schedule, the parents are already exercising continuous blocks of equal time, so a different designation of winter break may not be necessary.

The parents should also examine each other's work schedule during the break, as some parents may have extensive time off work during the break while others will be working full-time. The parents may want to consider agreeing on a schedule where the parent who doesn't have to work during the entire break will have the child more, and the parent who has a more demanding work schedule can maximize their time somewhere else. If a parent has to work during much of their break time, that parent will be expected to provide for childcare or a camp during any time they can't be present with a child who is too young to stay alone.

A sample Holiday Plan Chart is in Appendix 3.

Summer Break and Other Vacations

When a parent has designated summer vacation time with the child, that assignment of vacation time overrides the regular parenting schedule. A Plan should define whether vacations can be taken at any time of the year or just during the child's summer break from school. When a Plan is for a child that hasn't yet started formal school (kindergarten and above), the parents are usually free to take vacations at almost any time of year, but as soon as the child starts school, the ability to vacation during the school year is all but eliminated. This is particularly true as most Plans designate where the child will be during all scheduled school breaks. Vacations cannot be scheduled for spring, fall, or winter break when those breaks are already assigned in the Plan. Vacation plans cannot override specifically assigned holidays and special days.

Parents are encouraged to choose their summer vacation dates early in the year, such as around March 1 or April 1. If the parents are not required to choose vacation dates until May 1 or later, neither parent can effectively make summer childcare plans. If either parent wants the child to attend a camp or special program, those programs start to fill up in March or even earlier. Parents are encouraged to exchange their summer vacation dates by March 1 of each year so that summer childcare and camp arrangements can be made.

Most Plans provide that after the parents have exchanged their summer vacation dates, if the dates conflict or overlap, one parent's dates will prevail (have priority) in even-numbered years and the others in odd-numbered years. The parent who does not have priority that year will need to reschedule their dates that year, but that parent will have priority in choosing dates the next year.

A note about 4th of July. If the parents decide to list 4th of July as a special holiday that overrides the regular parenting time schedule, this selection will limit both parents' ability to schedule summer vacations. As an example: If Father is given the first right to choose his vacation dates during odd-numbered years, but Mother is given 4th of July in odd-numbered years, Father doesn't really have the ability to freely schedule his vacation dates, as he can't schedule a vacation over the 4th of July. The parents are encouraged to leave 4th of July out of the regular holiday list, as each parent is allowed to choose the 4th of July holiday as part of their vacation time during the designated years.

Parents must carefully consider their regular timesharing schedule when creating summer vacation provisions. If the vacation clause says that each parent gets a one-week vacation with the child each summer, can that week be tacked on to the regular parenting days to create a longer vacation (up to nine or twelve days total, where a 5/2/2/5 schedule is involved)? This is rarely the intention of the parents, so specific language that says that the child will spend a maximum of seven to fourteen days away from the other parent is a good idea if that's what the parents intend.

Where the regular parenting schedule during the school year is a 5/2/2/5 schedule, many parents change to an alternating week schedule for eight weeks during the summer months. This allows each parent to schedule vacations (one or more) during their four week-long periods with the child without any scheduling problems. All notice provisions for travel still apply, even if the travel takes place during regular parenting time so that the non-traveling parent always knows if the child is out of town. Even if the parents don't feel the child is old enough to go with an alternating week schedule during the school year, the few weeks in the summer is a nice change and require fewer exchanges of the child each week while also permitting each parent to put the child in camps or other activities during their weeks.

No Make-up Time

When a parent loses some parenting time because of the holiday schedule, there is no make-up time for that parent. Holidays are generally either shared or alternated. There is little, if any, actual "lost" parenting time. The same applies to vacations and breaks—those times that are allocated in the Parenting Plan are awarded to one parent, and no make-up time is given to the parent who would have had the child but for the break.

Let Go of "Equal"

Many co-parents try to make parenting time come out exactly equal. If the parents have a relatively equal parenting time schedule (like alternating weeks or a 5/2/2/5 schedule), the holiday and break schedule will often skew the days to favor one parent slightly more than the other. Attempts to have the number of parenting time days come out exactly equal each year will usually result in disputes and chaotic calendars. It's not reasonable to expect each and every year to result in 182.5 days of parenting time to each parent. In a given year, because of the break and holiday schedule, one parent may actually end up with 175 days and the other with 190 days. This could seem very unfair – that's more than two additional weeks with one parent! And yet, over a period of several years, the schedule will even out more and come closer to an equal division of days.

Parents may disagree with leaving certain holidays off the schedule, leaving them to fall where they may on the regular calendar. If a parent searches future calendars (sometimes years in the future), it could appear that most of those undesignated holidays naturally fall on the other parent's days, which doesn't seem fair. Those things are going to happen. Calendars are not perfect, and your child is not a timeshare. Attempts to exactly equalize parenting time days seem to be evidence of a parent's need to feel "equal" (or at least not to feel like a lesser person) and are not a legitimate emphasis on the child's best interests or needs.

J. Transitions (Exchanges) and Transportation

Exchanges of the child can be fraught with drama and conflict, or they can be uneventful. Many exchanges of the children are done through the school or at the childcare provider, meaning one parent drops the child off at school in the morning and the other picks them up to start parenting time after school, so the parents don't usually see each other. This is less stressful for the child who is in a natural state of transition and doesn't have to experience physically going from one parent to the other.

In this section, we'll consider issues that typically come up around exchanges.

Exchange Times

If a Parenting Plan has only referred to exchanges through school or at a childcare provider and an exchange suddenly must happen when school isn't in session unless the parents can agree otherwise, the exchange time should occur at the same time school would have started or ended. Ideally, a Parenting Plan should explain that exchanges will occur *"at the start of the school day, or if school is not in session, 8 am"* but if that language is not in the Plan, the parents need to agree if they want a different time than the usual school times.

Exchange Locations

School is not always open to handle the exchange. There are non-school days, holidays, and days when a child who didn't go to school has to be exchanged. If a specific location for an exchange is not stated in the Plan, the exchange usually takes place at the home of the parent who is giving up the child, on the theory that the parent who is picking up the child is likely to be prompt, and that location is more convenient for the child. The parents may agree to a different exchange location. The parent who is giving up the child may not, however, require the receiving parent to travel to a far-off location to pick up the child, such as "We will be at my sister's home" when the sister's home is a greater distance away than the residential parent's home. If a child is attending a scheduled activity at the time an exchange is to occur, then the receiving parent would be expected to pick up the child at the end of that activity as long as the parents agreed on that activity for the child.

Transportation of the Child

Your Plan may say who drives the child for exchanges. But if it doesn't, consider an easy default situation that for in-person exchanges (where the exchange is not being done by a school or childcare drop-off), the parent who is receiving the child does the driving. The parent who has the child at their home is expected to see that the child is ready at the exchange time with personal belongings that will be transferred, and the parent who is picking up the child is expected to arrive at the exchange location promptly.

Parent Communication and Demeanor During Exchanges

Parents must be on their best behavior at child exchanges to minimize stress to the child. Parents who prepare themselves mentally to be aware of their behavior are doing their child a great service.

Parents should not plan to exchange information or have lengthy discussions at exchanges. Exchanges should be for one purpose only:

helping the child transition from one parent to the other. While it's fine to exchange some of the child's personal belongings, a favorite toy, electronics, etc. (as those things are for the child's comfort), the parents should not exchange money, reimbursements, requests for reimbursements, paperwork, household items, or mail. The parents can make other arrangements to transfer those things when the child isn't present.

The parents should speak minimally to each other at the exchanges. If a warm greeting is possible, then a more pleasant general conversation is fine. If the parents are not able to exchange a genuinely warm greeting at an exchange, a formal "Hi, how are you?" is all that needs to be said. If a child has been ill, a quick exchange of how the child has been feeling, recent temperature or fever information, and mentioning the last time they slept or had medication is fine to discuss, as that's strictly about the child. Changes or proposed changes to the parenting schedule or proposals for an activity or a vacation are not to be discussed at exchanges or in front of the child.

The Child's Demeanor at Transitions

Possibly the most common thing family law professionals hear from parents is something like,

"There's something wrong at [other parent's] house. He hates going there. When I tell him [other parent] is on the way to get him, he cries." Or *"She tells me she doesn't want to go with [other parent]. I know she doesn't say that about me! Why should I have to force her to do something she doesn't want to?"*

A child being upset just before or during an exchange is completely normal. Children like to stay in one place and continue the activity they're involved in, and they don't like to be disrupted for change. The child at that moment of transition really does want to stay at the same place, and that desire has little to do with liking one parent or one household more than the other. It has to do with not wanting to be interrupted. (The same applies to interrupting a child's activities to force a scheduled phone call with the other parent.) When the other parent says later, *"He was fine once he got in the car/once we got home,"* that's likely the truth. Once the exchange happens, the child settles in and becomes comfortable with the new situation (and again, doesn't want that situation to change for the next transition either). Consider the child's demeanor when they're forced to get up in the morning earlier than they want to, for school or otherwise. Consider their reluctance to get ready for school, get dressed, or eat breakfast. These are the same types of behaviors that will arise at the time of exchanges that happen between the parents' homes, and the child's reaction to the exchanges doesn't indicate that something is "wrong" with the other parent or the other parent's household.

Curbside Exchanges

When the parents have had difficulties or hostilities during exchanges, it is best to have the parents not approach each other. This is accomplished by curbside exchanges, meaning the receiving parent remains in the car, parked curbside at the other parent's home, and the child walks from the front door to the car by themselves. This can only be done where a child is capable of walking themselves for a short distance with both parents watching for safety from a distance. The parent giving up the child will remain at the doorway and not exit the immediate area of that home's front door except to the extent necessary to ensure the child's safety. The receiving parent may exit the car if necessary to assist the child with belongings or a car seat.

For a child too young to walk alone from the front door area to the car, the parents must get closer to exchange the child. If curbside exchanges are a problem for these parents, selecting a public location for exchanges may be necessary. For those exchanges, the parents meet in a public parking lot, sometimes in a remote section of a shopping center that is not likely to be crowded, parking closely enough together so that the child is not exposed to traffic.

In some cases, court orders even have to be entered stating which parent removes the child from one car seat and puts the child into the other car seat. While those provisions are not usually necessary, that issue highlights how serious the conflict gets at some of the in-person exchanges.

Parents have been known to suggest that exchanges take place at police stations or police station parking lots. In general, if a child is old enough to know they're at a police station, that is not a good location for an exchange. A child should not be expected to equate a meeting of his parents with a visit to the police station. Some police station locations actively discourage the use of their stations for exchanges, noting that an auxiliary station may not be open and staffed during the hours the exchange is taking place. Grocery stores, fast food outlets, and restaurants tend to be well-lit, have longer hours, and often have security cameras, which promote safety for all at exchanges.

Persistent Tardiness for Exchanges

If one parent is accused of being persistently late for exchanges, the use of fast-food outlets can be helpful. Each parent can be instructed to purchase a nominal item (a small Coke) and keep the receipt showing the date and time of purchase as proof of when they arrived at the exchange location. If one parent is consistently late for an exchange, sanctions are appropriate to deprive that parent of parenting time in the future, and sometimes a "two-for-one" sanction is effective. For the parent who persistently brings the child late to an exchange, that parent loses two minutes of future parenting time for every minute they are late, so a late arrival of 20 minutes results in the loss of 40 minutes of future parenting time, and so on. For the parent who persistently arrives late to receive the child, that parent loses future parenting time, and the parent who is delivering the child may be allowed to leave (with the child) after a certain number of minutes. The person who arrived late to get the child will be required to drive somewhere else for pickup.

Another late arrival sanction can be monetary fines. Most childcare providers start charging extra fees for late pickups, and a parent who arrives more than 5 or 10 minutes after the scheduled time can be charged a few dollars per minute of tardiness. Childcare providers tend to charge at least $5 per minute.

It's helpful to find out the supposed reasons for the persistently late parent. If traffic or work hours are consistently cited as excuses, the exchange time should possibly be changed to reflect the problem. If persistently being late appears to be an issue of disorganization or disrespect for the other parent's time, using sanctions (limiting parenting time or requiring payment) may resolve the problem.

Third Parties at Exchanges

Unless the parents agree, having third parties at exchanges is rarely a good idea. If the third party is a new partner or a family member who has a history of conflict with the other parent, the third party has no business being anywhere near the exchanges. If the parents are in active litigation in court about anything (either parenting or money-related, etc.), it's likely that exchanges will be tense, and a third party's presence is likely to make things worse. If one parent believes having a third party present at the exchange is necessary for the parent's safety, rules should be implemented that the third party will remain in the vehicle and will not engage or speak to the other parent for any reason.

Occasionally, a third party's involvement makes things better. If one parent re-partners and that new partner is non-confrontational and even calming to the situation, a parent may prefer to do the exchange with the new partner. This is something that needs to be discussed on a case-by-case basis. The lack of trust between parents/ former partners sometimes does not extend to the new partner, and trust and respect make exchanges more comfortable for the child.

Helpful clauses for exchange issues, as described above, include:

Exchanges:

Whenever possible, exchanges of the child will be done through school or childcare, with one parent dropping the child off at school and the other parent picking the child up at the end of the school day.

When school/childcare cannot be used for an exchange (meaning a non-school day, holiday, or a day the child has not attended school), the parents will exchange the child at the residence of the parent who is ending parenting time unless the parents agree to a different location.

Either parent may designate a third party to handle the exchange transportation for the child, so long as the other parent is given no-

tice of the specific person who will be arriving to pick the child up.

Unless prohibited by court order, either party may have a third party accompany them to the exchanges so long as the third party does not leave the vehicle, does not approach the other parent, and does not speak to or communicate with the other parent in any way.

Curbside Exchanges:

If the parents are ordered to do residential curbside exchanges, they will occur at the home of the parent who is ending parenting time. That parent remains at the front door or close to the residence entrance and will not approach the other parent's car. The child will walk alone from the residence entrance to the receiving parent's car. The receiving parent may exit their car only to help the child with carrying items or to help into a car seat. The parents will not approach each other.

Exchanges at a public location:

If the parents are ordered to do exchanges at a public location, the exchanges will occur at the [name of business] located at [address] in the parking lot described as [_____]. During exchanges, there shall be no communication between the parents or anyone accompanying them. This means there shall be no gestures, no speaking, no signs, and no lengthy eye contact. The parents shall drive safely during exchanges and should not "peel out," skid their tires, or speed. Each parent shall always maintain a distance of at least 10 feet from the other parent and their accompanying adult during these exchanges. Each parent shall park their car at least 10 feet, but not more than 50 feet, from the other parent's car. The child shall move between the cars, but adults do not move with them. When the child is leaving a parent, they may be helped by that parent from the car, the trunk may be opened to remove items for the child, and that parent may give the child quick hugs/kisses. While this is happening, the receiving parent shall stay in their car. Then the child shall walk by themselves with their items to the receiving parent's *car. Immediately upon the child beginning their walk, the parent they are leaving shall re-enter their car and may leave or wait until the child is in the receiving parent's car. When the child arrives at the receiving parent's car, they may exit their car to help the child inside and open the trunk, as needed. Essentially, the parents should never both be outside of their cars at the same time. Exchanges shall be safe, fast, and uneventful.*

K. Travel with the Child

It's likely each parent is going to travel with the child, and how the travel plans are handled is very important in the co-parenting arrangement. The wording of the Plan depends on the type of travel involved.

We discuss the various issues involved in traveling with a child and propose some sample travel language at the end of this section.

Piggybacking

"Piggybacking" refers to a situation in which one parent schedules their vacation parenting time at the beginning or end of their regular parenting time, resulting in a significant extension of the other party's time away from the child. This occurs because parenting time is effectively added to vacation time, leading to an extended period during which the child is not in the care of the non-vacationing parent. It also results in the parent without annual preference losing vacation time or being forced to exercise vacation time on certain weeks due to a short summer break. As an example, if you share a week on/week off parenting time schedule and schedule your extra annual vacation week each year during the week you do not have the child, it is possible you will have three consecutive weeks of parenting time with the child. For some parents, piggybacking can lead to a great deal of conflict and missed parenting time. If this is a concern, an appropriate clause to address piggybacking might be:

*When planning summer vacation, neither parent shall engage in "piggybacking" resulting in a situation where parenting time and vacation is combined, and the child is away from the other parent **for a period of more than** 10 consecutive **overnights** of parenting time and vacation combined. Should either parent wish to schedule sum-*

mer vacation parenting time combined with regular parenting time, that exceeds 10 consecutive overnights away from the other parent over the summer, they must obtain written consent from the other parent.

Travel Within the Immediate Vicinity of Home with an Overnight Stay

When the child is to be staying away from the custodial parent's (CP) home for an overnight, whether with the parent or with someone else, the non-custodial parent (NCP) usually should be advised of where the child is spending the overnight. This might not always be required, and the parents can agree that notice doesn't have to be given to the other parent for sleepovers or overnights at a family member's home. But without this agreement, it's probably best if a parent is told where the child is sleeping, if not at the other parent's home (including sleepovers).

In-State Travel

The CP may choose to travel somewhere else in the state (province or region) during their parenting time. If it's not a formal "vacation" that requires notice to the other parent, does the other parent have to be told about the travel? Generally, yes, if it includes an overnight. Even if the travel takes place only on the CP's weekend, with no loss of parenting time to the other parent, the other parent should be advised where the child is sleeping. Detailed information about activities isn't usually necessary, but the non-traveling parent should be told where the child will be sleeping (an address or hotel name), the location of travel (i.e., Cleveland), and the method of travel. Examples of good notice provisions for travel are:

"We're making the 2-hour drive to Cleveland on Friday afternoon and will be at the Valley Ho Resort in Cleveland until check out on Sunday, then back home by about 6 pm on Sunday evening."

or

"We're on Southwest Flight 888, Los Angeles to San Diego, on Friday, July 6, and return flight Southwest 999 on Sunday, July 8; we are staying at the Mission Beach Inn on Mission Avenue."

Out-of-State Travel/Summer Vacations

During the vacation period which is assigned to each parent in the Plan, more advance notice is usually necessary because the travel or vacation will take some parenting time from the other parent. A common provision is that each parent is allowed to take 14 days of vacation each summer and that the travel dates must be exchanged by a certain date (March 1, for example). Usually, the only notification needed by that specified (early) date is to get the specific vacation dates on everyone's calendar. Notice of the specific plans, such as location, hotel, and flights, can come later, closer to the time of travel.

The due date for setting vacation dates is often too late to accommodate other summer plans for the child and the family. For example, if the date to exchange vacation dates between parents is May 1, neither parent will know when the other is taking vacation until May 1, so a parent can't make plans for other summer activities like camps and childcare. Often, by early May, child activities and camps are fully booked. If a parent booked a camp time for dates the other parent has now taken for vacation, the deposit money for camp will be lost. For this reason, the parents should closely examine whether an earlier date (such as March 1 or March 15) for exchange of vacation dates is better so that activities and childcare can be arranged for the non-vacation time periods.

A travel clause that can be helpful could be:

Summer vacation:

Each parent is entitled to 14 days of summer vacation time with the child, to be exercised in either two one-week increments or one two-week increment. Vacation days cannot be exercised in less than seven-day increments unless the parents agree.[44]

The parents will exchange the dates for their summer vacation time with the child each year no later than March 1. If the parents' dates conflict, then in even-numbered years, Father's vacation dates have priority, and in odd-numbered years, Mother's vacation dates have priority. The parent who does not have priority for dates has until March 10 to submit alternate dates for that year. The submission of vacation dates by March 1/March 10 does not have to include specifics regarding the vacation at that time.

Vacation days can be appended to regular parenting time days to create a longer period of vacation, so a seven-day vacation can be appended to regular parenting time to create a vacation time of up to 10 or 11 days. Vacation days cannot be scheduled to create a period of time where the child will be away from either parent for a period longer than 14 days unless the parents agree in writing.

The parent traveling with the child will provide the non-traveling parent with a detailed itinerary for each vacation not later than 14 days prior to the start of the vacation. The itinerary will include all locations the child will be traveling, the method of travel, flight names, flight numbers and times, if applicable, any other methods of transportation to be used, and the location(s) where the child will be sleeping at night.

The itinerary will include telephone numbers of all locations where the child will be sleeping or an affirmation that the parent's cell phone number will be available for the non-traveling parent to contact the child, and the cell phone number will be stated in the itinerary. If a parent's travel plans are finalized less than 14 days prior to commencement of travel, then notification of all travel information must be given as soon as the travel is finalized.

If either parent is traveling out of the [local] metropolitan area with the child for an overnight during their regular parenting time, the same itinerary information as listed above will be provided to the non-traveling parent before travel begins.

Travel During Winter Break

After a child is school-aged, a parent may want to travel during the child's winter break. One or both parents may have family and want to spend part of the winter holiday in another state. The parents must discuss:

- whether a parent can travel with the child during the winter break.
- how the winter break schedule will be altered to accommodate for travel.

Using a fairly standard winter break division, which is shown earlier in this chapter, the parent who has the first half of the break would be limited in the ability to travel for more than a short time because the child will have to be back to have time with the other parent on either Christmas Eve or Christmas Day. The parent who is assigned the second half of the break probably has more flexibility with travel as that parent may have a longer, uninterrupted time with the child before school resumes. Ideally, the parents can agree to a modification of the winter break schedule to allow a parent to travel (fly) with the child at least occasionally during this break. If the non-traveling parent is asked to skip either Christmas Eve or Christmas Day with the child to accommodate travel, that parent should be offered additional time with the child before travel commences and should be offered Christmas Eve and Day the following year.

Consider both sides:

Nicole: Parents should always see their children on holidays, even if it's just for a few minutes. There are so many family traditions they will miss!

Annette: Sometimes, the Plan must acknowledge that the child has relatives out of state and it's important to see those relatives. Because the winter break and Christmas holidays are usually alternated in some way, a parent can be assured of having the child in town at least every other year. During those alternate years, a parent may have to accept that the child will be gone for both Christmas Eve and Christmas Day in order to accommodate travel. The parent who won't see the child on one of those actual days will have sufficient time to celebrate before or after the actual holiday.

Every family is different. To some families, spending the actual day with a child is extremely important. Others recognize that the child's relationship with other family requires that the child travel some years. Parenting Plans need to recognize each family's values and priorities.

When Travel Notice Should be Given

Generally, as soon as a parent has made firm plans for travel (booked a hotel, booked a flight), the other parent should receive prompt notice. Many Plans will say that notice must be given a certain number of days before travel, such as 14 days prior; those specific advance requirements should be followed. If a trip is planned later than the advance notice period, such as a trip booked three days before departure, a trip notice to the other parent should be sent immediately upon booking.

Child Flying as an Unaccompanied Minor (UM)

The parents need to discuss when they agree that a young child may fly unaccompanied ("Unaccompanied Minor" or UM to most airlines), without an adult. Unaccompanied flights are often necessary for long-distance Parenting Plans and may also be necessary to allow a child to visit with other family members. Until the parents have discussed this issue and reached an agreement, neither parent should allow an unaccompanied minor flight, even if the child seems okay with it. All airlines post unaccompanied minor flight information on their websites, and most airlines will accept unaccompanied minors at age six and up. A few will not permit children to fly unaccompanied, and a few will also have different age limitations. There are specific fees and procedures for unaccompanied minor flights which involve an adult going all the way to the boarding gate with the child and remaining at the gate until the flight departs (the child cannot be left at the airport alone), and an adult with picture ID must be waiting for the child at the destination gate.

Depending on the age of the child, the parents may want to consult professionals who know the child, including psychologists, about the child's readiness for unaccompanied travel. Parents need to jointly determine how the issue will be discussed with the child to assess their readiness. If more than one child is involved, the older child's readiness is important. Also, consider any anxiety or stress that may be placed on the older child as the result of being responsible for the younger child on the flight.

Child Flying with a Third Party

If a parent needs a third party to fly with the child (such as a grandparent, family member, or close friend), generally, the parent who has custodial responsibility for the child can make that decision. The NCP generally does not have the authority to disapprove of a third party who flies with the child unless there is a specific reason as to why that third party is inappropriate. Much like a CP's responsibility to provide appropriate childcare during their parenting time, a CP with joint decision-making authority for the child is expected to exercise good parental judgment in determining who may fly with the child during their parenting time. The CP may wish to consider providing the third party with a letter that is often called a "child travel consent." There is no specific form for this consent (as of the time of this writing), but generally, this consists of a notarized letter that includes basic information about the child, the person the child is traveling with, travel details, and an authorization for the child to travel with the third party.

The majority of Plans do not restrict out-of-country/international travel from the United States. This means the decision about whether a child can travel internationally is left to the traveling parent's judgment. Some Plans specify that if a country is on the U.S. State Department's Do Not Travel list (a Level 3 or Level 4 country), travel with the child to those locations is specifically prohibited. Even without that language in the Plan, it is not hard to imagine that a court would restrict a child's travel to those locations deemed dangerous by the U.S. government.

Parents who are concerned about international travel may consider dividing the travel into different categories for ease of future travel decisions, such as:

International Travel Level I: Air travel to Mexican resort areas, Caribbean, or other cruises with U.S. stops may be presumably permissible without permission of the other parent, but with the normal notification procedures to the non-traveling parent.

International Travel Level II: Travel to countries with no U.S. State Department advisories. The parents may agree this travel is also permissible without permission, or may require permission from the non-traveling parent, with permission to not be unreasonably withheld.

International Travel Level III: Travel to countries with complete or partial travel advisories. Many Plans will specifically prohibit travel with a child to countries with a specified threat level stated by the U.S. government.

> *Parents are presumptively permitted to travel internationally with the children without written consent of the other parent, although notice is required as set forth in this Plan. Neither parent may travel to an international location that is the subject of a Level III or IV travel advisory from the U.S. State Department.*

or

> *In advance of any travel, parents must agree in writing if either parent wants to travel internationally with the child.*

Child's Passport

Whether or not the child has a passport at the time the parents separate, the parents need to discuss under what circumstances a passport will be obtained (or renewed) for the child, where the passport will be kept, and when the passport is released to a parent traveling out of the country with the child. If Parent A is holding the child's passport, a provision should be included that it will be released to Parent B at least 14 days prior to travel, as long as Parent B has provided all the travel information. If Parent A is the designated passport holder, then the passport is to be returned to Parent A for safekeeping within 14 days after the end of travel. Where there are multiple children, the parents sometimes agree that each parent will hold a different child's passport. In higher conflict co-parenting relationships, a provision that each parent holds the passport for a year at a time (i.e., Mother in even-numbered years and Father in odd-numbered years) may be necessary.

Passport and renewal applications require the signatures of both parents, although only one parent needs to accompany the child to the passport office. In the United States, the form required for children under age 16 is the DS-11 as of the writing of this book.

Parents should also discuss how the passport fee will be paid, whether it is split or paid entirely by the parent who is requesting the passport for specific travel. Parents are encouraged not to agree that passports will be retained in a jointly-held safe deposit box that requires both parents' signatures or keys to obtain them, as this method will require extensive cooperation and scheduling.

Sample passport language could be:

Passport application:

The parents will cooperate to obtain a passport for the child. Father will initiate the application and will supply Mother with a copy of the fully executed application along with Form DS 3053 for her signature. Mother will provide the fully signed form showing her consent, including her notarized consent, and Mother will supply Father with a copy of the front and back of her driver's license as required for the application.

Payment:

The parties will each pay 50% of the application fee - OR - Father will pay the application fee. Should Mother ever need to use the child's passport, Mother will reimburse Father for one-half of the application fee.

Possession of Passport:

The child's passport will be in the possession of Father during odd-numbered years starting in 2019 and in the possession of Mother during even-numbered years starting in 2020. Each parent will keep a photocopy of the passport in their own possession.

Exchanging the passport:

When a parent needs the passport, the parent will supply the other parent with an initial itinerary of the planned travel, including destinations and approximate dates of travel. At least 14 days prior to any travel that requires a passport, the traveling parent will provide the other parent with a final itinerary, including flight dates, times, flight numbers, and location(s) where the child will be sleeping each night, and confirmation of a telephone number where the child can be reached during travel.

When the traveling parent needs the passport during a period of time the passport is maintained by the other parent, the passport will be released to the traveling parent 14 days prior to departure, provided that the final itinerary of information has been provided to the non-traveling parent. The passport will be returned to the parent assigned to hold it within seven days after conclusion of travel.

Contact with the child during international travel:

Parent communication with the child during international travel will be scheduled for at least one call every third day of travel, to be coordinated between the parents based on the child's activities and itinerary. Should the parents not be able to agree, the child will call the non-traveling parent on the 4ᵗʰ, 7ᵗʰ, and 10ᵗʰ days of travel at 6 pm Arizona time for a brief (less than 10 minute) call.

L. First Right of Refusal

A provision commonly known as "first right of refusal" or "first right of caretaking" is sometimes included in a Parenting Plan. It's abbreviated here as "FROR." A FROR provision might look something like this:

CHILD CARE FOR CHILD AND FIRST OPPORTUNITY TO OTHER PARENT. When a parent has residential responsibility for the child, that parent will be responsible for providing childcare or supervision. If that parent is unable to care for the child for more than six consecutive hours, the other parent will be afforded the first opportunity to care for the child.

The number of hours that trigger the FROR can vary. The six-hour provision in the clause above is arbitrary. Some Plans use time periods as short as 2-4 hours or longer periods of time, such as overnights.

The clause is deceptively innocent. If the parent who is assigned parenting time with the child has to be away from the child for a given number of hours (say, six hours), some think it logical that the other parent should always be the first choice of caretaker (if available) before someone else gets to care for the child. Not necessarily. A FROR clause can lead to all kinds of problems, and for this reason, we suggest that you consider very carefully whether to include one in your Plan.

Some of the abuses of this provision include:

- A parent may insist that a child may not attend after-school, childcare, or camp while the CP is at work, because the NCP is available to take care of the child.

- A parent may say that a child cannot spend an overnight with a friend or relative because the CP will not be there, thus triggering the FROR clause.

- A parent could refuse to allow a child to spend any time with a stepparent or grandparents unless the CP is also in the same household.

Additional issues that can arise with a FROR clause include:

- Who will transport the child between households?

- What if the parent who wants the first right puts restrictions on their ability to take care of the child? Such as "Well, I get to take care of them, but as you'll be gone until at least 9 pm, they must stay overnight at my house, and you can pick them up the next morning."

- What if the NCP is asked to care for the child and doesn't respond with an unequivocal "yes"? An answer of "Well, maybe, I need to check on something," followed by a delay of several days, puts the CP in a bad position, as they are unable to make other childcare plans while waiting for a response. How long does the CP have to wait for an answer before calling a babysitter?

- What if the CP's family (grandparents, aunts, uncles, etc.) could easily care for the child at the CP's home to minimize disruption to both the child and the parent?

Unfortunately, the FROR clause is so frequently misused and abused that it has become much more about the parents and their disputes than what's best for the child. The situation to enforce FROR often comes up in stepparent or grandparent situations, where one parent seeks to prevent a stepparent or grandparent from having any alone time with a child when the CP is unavailable.

The benefits of a child being cared for by someone other than a parent could include:

- The child may be able to remain in the CP's home and won't require transportation and exchanges;

- The child can develop relationships with extended family, including grandparents, aunts, uncles, and cousins, through extended stays or sleepovers;

- The child can develop social relationships through extended stays or overnights with friends;

- The child develops social relationships and makes friends by attending formal childcare or after-school care with others;

- The child can rely on the schedule and routine of being in one parent's house on certain days without experiencing back-and-forth or possibly confusing schedules;

- The parents don't have to resolve the sometimes-complicated issues of who must provide transportation each way for the child;

- If a parent's night out ends after the child's bedtime, the child (left at home with a 3rd party caretaker) can go to sleep in their own bed; and

- The parent who has custodial time can ask a paid care provider to do other things at the parent's home, like housework, preparation of meals, and homework help.

Consider both sides:

Nicole: FROR causes unnecessary conflict, devalues important 3rd party caregivers, and forces parents to account for their whereabouts at all times when they have the children.

Annette: FROR has its place if the parents are able to work together and especially in situations where one parent has unusual work hours or travels often. Also consider keeping it for children under the age of 3, at least for longer periods of time like eight hours or more.

The FROR clause probably started out with good intentions. It has unfortunately been misused by some parents to the point that it has become more of a means to fight with the other parent rather than do what is best for the child. Contrary to some people's beliefs, it simply can't be said that a child is *always* better off being cared for by a parent than by anyone else. If that were true, a child might never attend formal school or take part in extracurricular activities.

Consider that if a Parenting Plan doesn't have this clause, each parent is still free to choose to call the other parent when childcare is required. Agreement is always possible. It's the forcing of the issue and the requirement to ask the other parent first that has caused the problems described above.

Is this clause ever a good idea? With children younger than five or six years old, and particularly with infants and toddlers, the clause can make sense if it applies to the CP being gone for an overnight. The clause could be written in a less restrictive way that leaves some discretion to the CP.

CHILD CARE FOR CHILD AND FIRST OPPORTUNITY TO OTHER PARENT. When a parent has residential responsibility for the child, that parent will be responsible for providing childcare or supervision. If the custodial parent is unable to care for the child for an overnight period of time, the other parent will be offered the first opportunity to care for the child for the overnight period during the hours the custodial parent is unavailable. When the custodial parent makes the offer of caretaking, the noncustodial parent will respond with a definitive "yes" or "no" to the offer within 24 hours of receiving the offer. The failure of the noncustodial parent to communicate an unequivocal "yes" within 24 hours will be considered to be a negative response, and the custodial parent will, in that case, be permitted to obtain their own third-party childcare. The first right of caretaking does not apply to a child who will be spending an overnight with friends or family members.

CHAPTER 6

Telephone Calls Between Child and Parent

The parent who doesn't have the child usually wants to talk to them on the phone (or Facetime) at some point while the child is at the other parent's home. Having some interim contact while the child is with the other parent can be important to maintain a connection between the NCP and the child, especially for young (preschool and early elementary-aged) children. Too much communication, however, can cause problems for the child.

There is a wide variation in how often the NCP and the child should communicate, and that depends on many factors, including the child's age and maturity level, the level of conflict between the parents, the child's activities and schedule, and the parenting schedule. In this chapter, we'll help you think through your options and draw up a Plan that will work for your child and for you and your co-parent.

A. Types of Contact

Parents should consider the type of contact that each will have when they are the NCP. Types of contact include:

- telephone
- Facetime, Skype, Zoom, Meet, Facebook Messenger, or other online visual conferencing services
- text and direct messaging
- social media and video games with messaging

The parents should discuss which of these types of contact will be allowed and which are preferred. Texting, social media, and gaming messaging will start to become available for preteens and teens. Constant messaging or texting can be intrusive on the CP's time and household rules, so putting reasonable limits on texting with the NCP may be advisable.

Problems arise when communication between the NCP and the child encroaches on and actively interferes with the CP's time. It can also be a problem if communication conflicts with the child's activities, sleep, or homework time. Parents may disagree on what types of communication are appropriate, particularly when texting is involved. Parents may disagree about whether the "quality" of the contact is sufficient because sometimes calls take place in a moving vehicle or in a public place, or the child may be in a room with other people with lots of background noise during the call.

A common clause about communication in a Parenting Plan might be something very simple, like:

The child shall be allowed to telephone the other parent as they wish, within reason

or

The child and the NCP will have reasonable telephone communication

Some Plans go into more detail by specifying that the NCP and child may text or have Facetime or other online chats. The frequency and duration of these contacts can be challenging areas.

Review your Parenting Plan to find out if these specifics are covered:

1. Are there set times and days of the week for phone calls? Should there be a set schedule or should it be any time that is reasonable? Are the parents capable of agreeing on what is reasonable?

2. Can a parent call at any time? Can the child call the other parent at any time?

3. Who is to dial the call? The child, the CP or the NCP? What phone numbers will be used?

4. What if someone (parent or child) can't be available at the set call time?

5. What if the CP and child are out to dinner or at a public place at the call time?

6. Should calls be allowed if the child is riding in a car?

7. Is the child old enough to handle the calls on their own, or does the CP have to remain in the room to hold the phone or other device?

8. Can the call be placed on speaker? Can calls be recorded?

9. What about calls when the CP and child are traveling or on vacation? What if they're in a different time zone?

B. Frequency of Contact

The parents should discuss and decide if there will be a set call schedule. A schedule has both benefits and drawbacks. A schedule will likely interfere at some point with the child's activities in the CP's household. If a telephone schedule is used, the parents need to recognize that sometimes the child will not be available for the call at the specified time, and some backup provisions are necessary.

Some parents request daily telephone contact with the child. Whether or not a daily call is needed by the child should be examined, as it may be too intrusive at times. If the parents are following a relatively equal parenting schedule with fairly frequent exchanges (a 5/2/2/5 or a 2/2/3), it's likely that a child doesn't need to speak with the NCP every day, as they will be seeing each other soon. If the parents have an alternating week parenting schedule and the child isn't yet high school age, one or two calls to the NCP during the week is likely enough for the child to maintain contact.

Too often, frequent or daily phone calls are scheduled and the frequency is for the benefit of the parent, not the child. When a child is showing consistent reluctance to making scheduled phone calls to the other parent, the parents should find a way to determine what frequency of contact the child needs and should adjust the calling requirements accordingly.

Once children are in high school or close to it, they should have more leeway in when and how to contact the NCP. Forcing a child of age 12 or older to follow a strict call schedule with the NCP is usually unnecessary. Our suggested telephone clauses anticipate that the child is old enough to manage their own contact with the NCP, and requests to speak with the NCP should be allowed at any reasonable time.

In general, if the CP is putting a limit on the child's use of texting and messaging with school friends, then those same limitations can be applied to a child's contact with the NCP outside of the set call schedule. But if a child is permitted unfettered access to friends' texts and online communications without limits, then the CP can't reasonably limit the child's communications only with the NCP. That means the child is restricted only from talking to the other parent but not from anyone else in the world. If the CP's household rules state that there will be no use of devices from 6-8 pm during dinner and homework time, then those rules may also logically apply to the child's unscheduled contact with the NCP.

C. Environment for Child's Telephone and Facetime (or Other Virtual) Calls

The location of the child and their privacy during the calls should be discussed. For a child who is old enough to handle the phone, iPad, or other device on their own, a privacy clause should be included to specify that no adult will monitor the child's call with the other parent. A child who is not old enough to hold the device (iPad or other type of tablet) or phone by himself on their own will require the presence of the CP to dial and/or hold the device; there's little way around that until the child can handle the call by themself. Without the CP present, the child could hang up on the call, drop the device, or start wandering around the house holding the device, which doesn't usually make for a good-quality call.

D. Important Guidelines for Parents

Provisions we believe are important in a general telephone access clause:

- The child should be given privacy for the calls, and no adult should overhear or monitor the child's calls with the other parent.

- The child should not be used to transmit messages from one parent to the other during calls.

- Neither parent will attempt to speak with the other parent during the child's calls.

- A timer or alarm should not be set for calls.

- The calls should not intrude on the CP's privacy. The child should not be permitted to take an iPad or another visual device around the CP's home, with the exception of the child's own bedroom.

E. A Sample (Very Specific) Phone Call Clause

Unless the parents agree otherwise, the child will have telephone contact with the NCP on the following schedule: On Tuesdays, Thursdays, and Saturdays between 6:45-7 pm Arizona time. The CP is responsible for seeing that the child initiates the call to the NCP during that time frame. These calls will not be made from a vehicle, and the child will be given privacy for the duration of the call. Neither parent will record the child's calls with the other parent. If the NCP is not going to be available to take a call during that time, they will notify the CP of that fact in advance, and the call will not be rescheduled. If the CP cannot make the child available for a call during a scheduled time, they will notify the NCP of that fact ahead of time, and the call will be rescheduled if possible. The call may last up to 10 minutes in duration. This call schedule may be modified during vacation and break periods when the child is traveling in order to accommodate the trav-

el, but the child will have telephone contact with the non-traveling parent at least once every three days of travel. The child will be permitted to call the NCP at other reasonable times if the child requests. "Telephone contact" or "call" as used in this clause includes Facetime contact.

A clause for telephone contact with a very young child might include the following:

The parents recognize that Allison is four years old and unable to stay on calls or video calls for very long. It is therefore agreed that the calling parent's contact with Allison will be limited to 3-5 minutes per session, to take place between 7:15 and 7:30 pm, shortly before her bedtime.

F. Parent and Child Interactions at Special Events

The parent who is assigned parenting time that day (the CP), or someone designated by the CP, should take the child to activities, school, and the like. Sometimes, both parents will be present at a special event or activity. That could be the case for a school program, field trip, game or tournament, recital, or a class party where parents are invited. Ideally, parents will communicate in advance about any events where they both may be present. If both parents are attending an event, they should make some minimal arrangements so there are no surprises, especially for the child. Advance planning between the parents will keep the child's stress level to a minimum during these joint events.

When in the same place, parents should be respectful and civil to each other for the sake of the child and to reduce the child's embarrassment. If there are no restraining orders, then a simple greeting, smile, or wave between co-parents may be appropriate, but substantive conversation should be avoided. This will reduce stress for the child and alleviate anxiety at the possibility of parental conflict. At the event, the child should be permitted to greet both parents, but the child should spend most time with, and return home with the parent who has parenting time that day.

Example of advance planning between parents:

"I'll be at the Winter Celebration program at Lincoln School on Thursday. It's your time with Chris, so I know you'll be bringing him to and from the program. He will know I'm there, and I would appreciate being able to say hi to him. We will talk for no more than five minutes, and I'll send him back to sit with you/your family after that, as it's your parenting time."

or

"The soccer playoffs are all day on Saturday, and as it's my day, I'll be taking Allie to the games at Frontier Park. When she's not playing, I'll send her over to say hi to you for a few minutes, but she will know that she's to return to sit with us for most of the games. I would appreciate you backing me up on that, and if she hangs around at your seat for more than five minutes or so, remind her to return to us. Thanks in advance. Her team is doing outstanding this year."

No matter how high the level of conflict is between parents, the child is likely going to need some level of contact with the parent they aren't living with at the time. Especially for very young children, a brief telephone or video connection with the absent parent can be comforting. The parents should recognize that if an older child is consistently showing irritation with being interrupted for a scheduled phone call with the NCP, it may be time to reduce the number of phone calls. At a certain age, probably the age when a child is trusted with their own cell phone, the child can be given the responsibility to contact the NCP when they feel it necessary, with an occasional gentle reminder from the CP to call the NCP once in a while.

CHAPTER 7

Child Medical Care Decisions

Your Parenting Plan should adequately cover important medical, dental, psychological, and health issues. Many divorced or separated parents engage in joint legal decision-making (JLDM), meaning the parents make big medical decisions together. This may also be called joint custody.

When a parent has the child for regular parenting time, however, that parent must make day-to-day decisions like how sick is a child, should they stay home from school, what over-the-counter medications should be given, is a trip to the pediatrician or Urgent Care needed? Only rarely does a residential parent need the other parent's permission to provide this kind of routine, day-to-day care for a child.

Major health and medical decisions, on the other hand, are to be decided jointly where the parents have JLDM. This is different from the day-to-day decisions that the residential parents make, such as whether to give the child an Advil for a headache or keep the child home from school with a cold.

Regarding medical issues, the Plan should cover at least these health-related things:

- Make sure the definition of "health" or "medical" care includes decisions about mental health, dental, and optical care, as well as decisions about what we consider "regular" medical. Each parent should understand that health or medical care is broadly defined and includes things like whether the child receives chiropractic or naturopathic care.

- The Plan should include the names of all medical professionals currently treating the child, with a provision that new medical professionals will not be substituted unless agreed to by both parents.

- The Plan should specify who is responsible for taking the child to well-child treatments like checkups, sports physicals, vaccinations, teeth cleaning, and other routine matters. The Plan may specify that the parents alternate taking the child to these appointments or that one parent is responsible for all appointments for one child and the other parent takes the other child. No matter which parent takes the child to an appointment, both parents are entitled to full medical information about the child.

- If a medical provider's office includes access to a portal (an online account with access to medical information, including office visit notes and test results), both parents should have the login information for the child's portal. The parents need to check with the child's pediatrician or Primary Care Provider (PCP) to see if the practice offers an online portal where all the child's records are uploaded after each appointment. The use of a health portal will simplify the child's records, which will ensure both parents have the same accurate and timely information about the child's health care. If the PCP practice does not provide an online portal, then the parent who takes the child to each appointment should be required to provide the other parent with all information and paperwork from the appointment within 24 hours of the appointment.

- Each parent should be allowed to give a child routine over-the-counter medications that the parent deems necessary during their parenting time. An email should be sent to the other parent at the time of an exchange so the other parent knows what medications the child has been taking, and when.

- If the child is taking prescription medication, all information about the medication should be exchanged in writing. Each parent should confirm that the CP will administer prescribed medications and treatments in accordance with doctor's orders. The parents will need to coordinate where the prescription is filled and which parent will pick it up.

- A Plan that addresses the above-listed items will go a long way towards preventing misunderstandings and arguments between parents on medical issues. The child's safety requires that the parents cooperate and exchange medical information consistently and accurately.

A. Routine Medical Care, Check-ups, and Scheduling Appointments

Children need well-care doctor visits, including relatively minor appointments for things like teeth cleaning or adjustment of braces. These could be called "routine" appointments. The Plan should state whether the parents are going to share taking the child to those routine appointments. Or, one parent might be in charge of scheduling all appointments, and that parent will need to immediately upload all appointment information to a shared calendar so the other parent knows what's going on. If the parents are alternating who takes a child to routine appointments, parent communication is necessary to make sure appointments are not missed or duplicated. If the parents are alternating taking the child, then each parent will schedule their own appointments as they know their own availability. The Plan should state that when a parent makes an appointment, only that parent can reschedule or cancel the appointment.

Attendance at Medical Appointments

The Plan should state, or the parents should discuss, who will attend the routine appointments. Do both parents plan to attend all routine well-check appointments, teeth cleanings, and braces adjustments? If so, why? Can any third party attend the appointments (including a new spouse or significant other, a grandparent, or a nanny)? Can anyone other than a parent take the child to a routine appointment? If the parents can't agree on these things, the presumptive limitation should be that only a parent—not a stepparent or grandparent—can take a child for health care. Most medical practices will require this. In general, no third parties, no matter what the relation, can attend the child's appointments unless both parents agree.

Unfortunately, medical practices have been known to "fire" patients and discontinue treating the child if parents and stepparents cannot get along or cause a scene while at appointments. If parents are so hostile that they get into disputes in a medical office, a prohibition for joint attendance should be implemented. Some medical practices might allow a second parent to attend telephonically or remotely, but those requests should be reserved only for serious medical issues, and some medical practices will not have the ability to schedule one parent remotely when the child is there in person.

Choice of Child's Primary Care Provider (PCP)

Because the PCP is integral to helping parents resolve disputes about the child's medical care, the choice of this provider is important. In high-conflict cases, parents have been known to take the child to two different PCPs, which can result in duplicative care and a lack of information and coordination of care. Most doctors do not want to be in that position. If parents find themselves unable to agree on one primary care provider, the issue may be left to the court, or the parties can agree to use one care provider for one year and a different one the next.

If the parents have already chosen the child's PCP at the time of their separation, that provider and the name of the medical practice should be included in the Plan so it's clear who the child's PCP is.

Special Health Conditions and Specialists

The parents need to discuss who will attend the child's specialist or non-routine appointments. These appointments may involve a higher level of care and specific instructions that will be important for both households. These are the types of appointments that, if at all possible, both parents should attend.

Vaccinations

If the parents have JLDM and they cannot agree on whether a child is to receive a vaccination, the court (sometimes with a recommendation from a professional) can, in most jurisdictions, make the decision for them. Or, preferably, the court may enter orders stating which parent is in charge of vaccination decisions in order to resolve the dispute. When the parents disagree on vaccinations, the opinion of the child's PCP will often be requested, and the parents are encouraged to allow the PCP to make the final decision.

Testing and Medications; Second Opinions

When testing is requested by the child's PCP or a specialist, it's likely to be considered "reasonable and medically necessary" treatment. If a parent disagrees with recommended testing or medications, that parent usually will be allowed to get a second opinion from another qualified medical doctor, so the testing or medication may be delayed for a reasonable time to allow for the second opinion. The parent requesting the second opinion is usually responsible for the cost of that opinion. If the second opinion does not recommend the same testing or medication, and the parents cannot agree on a compromise position, the issue may also be left to the court, which may be forced to designate one parent as the final decision-maker to resolve the issue.

Sample second opinion language could be:

If either parent wishes to obtain a second opinion as to any health care issue (including medical, dental, orthodontic, psychological, vision, or eye care), the following procedure will be followed: The parent seeking the second opinion will notify the other parent; the parent seeking the second opinion will select the professional at their own expense (less any insurance coverage), after providing notice to the other parent. The child will be taken to the second opinion appointment during the requesting parent's parenting time; both parents are permitted to attend the second opinion appointment, and the second opinion doctor will be provided with all relevant medical or other records regarding the health care issue. If after receiving the second opinion, the parents are still unable to agree on a health care procedure, the issue will be submitted to the Parenting Coordinator or the court for final resolution.

> *Parent disagreements about certain medications, including those for ADD, anxiety, or depression, are not uncommon. Compromises can sometimes be reached with the help of a skilled specialist or the PCP. Medications can be given on a trial basis, with both parents meeting with the doctor in a specific time period to discuss how the child seems to be responding. Alternatives to medication management, such as behavior modification, change of home environment, and counseling, are also valid alternatives.*

Braces

Parents often disagree about whether braces are necessary, or if the need is obvious, when they should be put on. Braces are another area where a second opinion may be sought when the parents disagree. If disfigurement of the teeth is radical and affects a child's self-esteem or causes other medical issues, early braces may be called for. If braces are to be installed purely for cosmetic reasons or for minor misalignment, they may be able to wait until the child is older.

Notice Of Illness, Medications, and Appointments

When it comes to the child's medical treatment of any type, communication and notice between the parents is crucial. Whatever methods the parents have chosen for their communications, all information about appointments, medical treatment, providers' names and locations, diagnoses, recommendations, testing, and medications must be transmitted between the parents in writing. Most information should be uploaded to a shared calendar, and the use of a shared portal for all information (such as Our Family Wizard discussed in Chapter 4) makes the exchange of that information easier than sending individual emails. Important information about a child's medical care should be exchanged using calendars, portals, and emails and not put in texts, where the information can be misunderstood and easily lost.

B. Child Therapy and Parents' Participation

Whether a child needs therapy and the selection of a therapist are common areas of disagreement between parents. Some parents disagree with counseling in general, thinking that it means something is "wrong with" the child or the family, or out of fear that it might be used against them somehow in court. Other parents might want to jump into counseling for a child when something fairly routine in the child's development occurs.

When considering whether a child needs some short-term therapy in a separated parents' situation, note that resilient children can learn to function properly and even well in two different households, even those with radically different sets of rules and expectations, when they have the proper support. Other children who are not so resilient will suffer by going between two households and may always feel more "at home" or comfortable in one home over the other. If therapy can help your child move to a better point of resiliency by learning coping mechanisms and boundaries with the parents, the child's therapy can help to improve the overall Parenting Plan.

A common theme in high-conflict family cases is that the children end up in therapy when the issues would more properly be addressed by the parents in co-parenting counseling. Because the parents so rarely recognize their own (individual and joint) responsibility in family disputes, the children are often forced into counseling to gain the skills necessary to navigate their parents' hostility.

Generally, counseling should be viewed as a positive activity for children, as it allows them an outlet for concerns and teaches them how to develop boundaries and cope with co-parenting conflict. Parents should consider the therapist's skill level and experience in dealing with a child from a divorced or separated home. Parents should also steer clear of unlicensed "life coaches" who are engaging in a form of unregulated therapy with no accountability. All potential therapists should be asked about their experience in treating children of divorced and separated parents.

A Parenting Plan should include certain provisions in the event parents agree to therapy for the child or if they may need to agree on therapy for the child in the future. Parenting Plan considerations include:

- Who will provide therapy? If the parents cannot agree, then the method for selecting a therapist should be described. Parents may ask the child's pediatrician to make a recommendation along with possible recommendations from a child's school, or they may provide a list of names to the court for selection.

- How will expenses related to therapy be paid? Depending on the jurisdiction, therapy expenses may be considered medical expenses and may be divided in the child support order. Parents may want to request that a therapist be covered by insurance.

- How will parents communicate with the therapist? If there is a great deal of parental mistrust and concern about one parent's motivation for therapy, the parties may want to discourage or eliminate phone calls or texts between one parent and the therapist. Instead, the parents can create and jointly use one email account to communicate with the therapist and their staff, ensuring that both parents see all communications. This method can encourage transparency. If the therapist has a portal, the parents should share all login information to jointly access the portal.

- The frequency, mode, and duration of therapy? Depending on the parties' position on child therapy, especially if there is a concern about one parent terminating therapy, being alienated from therapy, or not taking the child to therapy, the Plan should include specifics as to how therapy will proceed. Many times, the best approach is to simply leave it up to the therapist to determine when therapy will take place, as well as when therapy is no longer needed as therapeutic goals are reached.

Sample language for orders appointing a child's therapist with boundaries built in to avoid misuse of the therapy process could read as follows:

The parties have agreed that (insert name) shall provide therapy to the child, [Or, the parties shall select a therapist from a list provided by their pediatrician, and with consideration of which therapist is available and covered by insurance.]

1. To ensure both parents receive all information and are equally permitted to engage with the therapist, the parties shall avoid substantive in-person or phone conversations with the therapist unless the other parent is present. The parties shall provide a copy of this report to the therapist and direct the therapist to communicate with them only through the following procedure.

i. All forms and communications to/from the therapist and staff should be sent/received by both parties at an agreed upon shared email address (hereinafter "therapy email"), such as john-therapy1@gmail.com (this is just an example). Mother shall create this therapy email address and provide the login information to Father, and she will ensure it is working for both parties by a date certain,

ii. Absent a written agreement, the parties shall not erase any therapy email messages or change the password for the therapy email address.

iii. A party will sign their name at the bottom of all emails sent to the therapist/staff from the therapy email. The parties may also copy their personal email for record-keeping purposes but may not use it to communicate with the therapist or staff.

iv. The parties shall check the therapy email on a daily basis.

v. The therapy email address shall be connected to any child therapist's health portal, if one exists. Further, if there is a child therapist's health portal, it will always be accessible and used by both parties, which means there will be one username/password that will be shared and used by both parties. If the child therapy portal is used for communication with the therapist/staff instead of the child therapy email address, the parties shall follow the same communication rules as set forth herein.

2. *The parties shall cooperate with the child's therapist and provide all information requested within 72 hours of the date/time sent to the therapy email. The parties shall share with each other any forms/releases they complete for the therapist. They shall do this by copying the therapy email address when they return the forms so the email appears in the inbox, allowing the other party to view it.*

3. *The therapist alone shall determine the frequency, duration, and mode of therapy for the child. Unless otherwise specified and conveyed in writing by the therapist to both parties using the therapy email, therapy sessions are to be conducted in-person a minimum of twice per calendar month ideally with each parent being responsible for scheduling and ensuring transportation to therapy sessions at least once a month.*

4. *The parties shall endeavor to collaborate and cooperate in the scheduling of therapy sessions, share the dates/times of all therapy sessions upon scheduling, and attempt to schedule therapy sessions in a manner that minimizes interference with the child's school day and academics. It is anticipated that the parents shall alternate responsibility for transporting the child to and from therapy or alternate hosting video-therapy sessions; however, it is understood that is not always possible given the availability of the parents, the child, and the therapist.*

5. *Video-therapy sessions may be conducted with the child present at either parent's home. Both parents shall provide the child with a working device with a camera, as well as a quiet, unmonitored, unsupervised, and uninterrupted space to engage in video-therapy sessions with the therapist.*

6. *Parents and/or the child shall not record therapy sessions without written permission from the therapist.*

7. If the therapist wishes to have a parent present and engaged in a specific session, the therapist shall convey this request in writing to both parties using the therapy email. If the therapist's written request is made in a timely manner, the requested parent may join the therapy session. Otherwise, only the parent responsible for scheduling and transporting the child to therapy may attend an appointment and should wait outside of the session.

C. Safe Haven Counseling for a Child

The parents may agree to, or a court may order something called "safe haven" counseling for a child. Generally, if safe haven counseling is undertaken, it is the intent of the parents or the court that the child has a counselor who cannot be compelled to testify at court about what the child has said in counseling sessions and the counselor's records of those sessions cannot be subpoenaed by either parent. The reasoning for safe haven status is that the child should have a safe place to talk about their concerns and problems without worrying that everything they say will end up in court or known by the parents. It preserves the therapist-patient privilege for the child.

Parents may want to ask their child's therapist questions about the use of safe haven therapy in their particular situation, specifically:

- Can the parents be prevented from getting access to their own child's counseling records?

- What will the therapist do if one parent wants the child's records released, and the other doesn't?

- What if a parent wants to use the child's therapy records for an improper purpose that doesn't have anything to do with helping the child?

A written agreement spelling out everyone's understanding of a safe haven counseling arrangement is the best way to ensure your child has privacy in a counseling relationship. Often this agreement will be provided by the counselor before the counseling starts, so that everyone knows the ground rules for the sessions.

A safe haven agreement should have at least the following provisions:

- The therapist should be permitted to communicate with the parents (or the court) if the therapist believes it's appropriate, about treatment and the purposes and goals of treatment.

- The therapist will determine the process, meaning who should be involved with the treatment and when. The therapist should be able to request sessions that include one or both parents if the therapist thinks it's necessary to help the child.

- The therapist should be required to provide the parents with treatment goals and, if requested, a treatment summary that does not infringe on the child's privacy.

- The therapist should be the one to determine when and if to share or discuss an issue with the parents. The parents should not be able to demand to know what's going on in the child's sessions.

- Neither the parents nor the parents' attorneys shall have access to information about the content of the therapeutic process. That means the child's therapist-patient privilege is preserved.

- The parents should agree not to subpoena the therapist's file or subpoena the therapist to a deposition or for trial testimony.

- The therapist should agree to speak with a court-appointed custody evaluator or another type of professional appointed by the court to assist the family relationship (this could be a therapeutic interventionist, the parents' counselors, or a parenting coordinator).

- The child's therapy can end if both parents agree in writing.

- If the therapist receives documents, emails, or letters from one parent, all those documents must be copied to the other parent at the same time.

A safe haven agreement should not, in the opinion of these authors, have these types of provisions:

- That the therapist will not talk to the parents at all.

- That the therapist may speak with a parent only if the other parent is present and may never speak with an individual parent.

- That the therapist may not be subpoenaed to trial or deposition to speak about the therapist's communications with the *parents* or *third parties*. (This is important because the therapist's communications with the parents or third parties are NOT protected by the child's privilege.)

- That the therapist will not speak with a court-appointed evaluator or court-appointed professional who is working with the family.

- That the therapist will not provide a treatment summary.

- That the therapist is not permitted to report abuse. (In most states, the law would require the therapist to report abuse.)

Unfortunately, it's not uncommon for a possibly well-meaning therapist to use safe haven orders as a shield against speaking to anyone about the course of the child's therapy. If that happens, the parents and the court should be prepared to challenge the therapist and narrowly define the safe haven orders so they cover only what is necessary to protect the child/patient from substantial harm.

To be clear: Safe haven orders are NOT primarily for the protection of the therapist or to shield the therapist from liability or from legitimate questions about the course of therapy. Safe haven orders should protect only detailed records and detailed information gained directly from the child's therapy. Safe haven orders are for the protection of your child, not the professional.

A sample safe haven clause for a child's therapy could be:

The parents have agreed that child's therapy with _____ will be safe haven therapy, meaning they understand that they will not have access to child's specific statements and confidences revealed in the therapy sessions, nor will they participate in the therapy sessions. The parents agree that child's therapy shall be a safe space for child to express concerns and confidences without fear that the parents will learn of the child's statements or misuse the statements. The parents agree that they will both sign the therapist's form of Safe Haven (or similar) documentation, which preserve their child's rights of confidentiality in therapy, and if necessary, they will consent to the entry of court orders establishing the safe haven therapy status. The parents understand that this agreement does not override the requirement that the therapist report any suspected child abuse or neglect pursuant to state law.

If the therapist refuses to speak with the parents at all, citing safe haven orders, the orders are being misused. If this is occurring, hopefully, the parents can reach an agreement that either the therapy orders or the therapist must be changed.

A child's therapist may wish to speak only with the parents when both parents are present. While individual discussions are fine for routine matters, like scheduling appointments or arranging payments, substantive information about the child should be communicated to both parents, and the parents should be treated as equally as possible by the therapist. When a therapist has substantive information for the parents, such as how a particular situation with the child could be handled or how to present a united front on a particular issue, that information should ideally be communicated to the parents at the same time and in the same way (i.e., either a joint meeting or an email).

A therapist should provide, if requested, a treatment summary that includes the child's treatment goals. The treatment summary and goals are not precluded in safe haven therapy. A treatment summary and designation of treatment goals are integral parts of the child's treatment. Sharing this information with the parents should not cause substantial harm to the child. In the unusual situation where a therapist feels merely revealing the treatment summary or treatment goals could be harmful to the child, the therapist should be prepared to substantiate that finding to the parents (and to the court if necessary) with specific information.

CHAPTER 8

Safety Decisions

Every parent worries about a child's safety. You and your co-parent may have similar philosophies about safety considerations, or your opinions may be very different. Some parents support having a child take risks, while the other parent is entirely risk-averse and feels it's very important to protect the child from most risks. Some of the safety concerns we address here are covered by specific laws or rules, and where those exist, that provides a baseline for how the child should be kept safe. Where there are no specific laws regulating a certain activity, parents will need to make individual choices for their child.

A. Car Seats

The use of car seats is one of a few parental safety decisions that:

- is not discretionary on the part of a parent.
- is fairly well-defined in the law
- can be enforced by the court.

Thus, the Parenting Plan for car seats and other vehicle restraints should be to follow the applicable laws.

Parents have a responsibility to be informed about child restraint laws in their home state and in any area where they'll be traveling with the child. Several websites consolidate the various states' or jurisdictions' laws on child restraints. Those sites show when a restraint is required, including the child's age, height, and weight, what type of restraint is required, when or if a child must be seated in a rear seat, and when a child can start using a regular seat belt. One example, at the time of this writing, is that in Arizona, a child who is under five years of age must be in a restraint regardless of the child's height. A child between the ages of five and eight who is taller than 5' need not be in a child restraint.

The proper installation of car seats and restraints is an important issue, and a parent may be justified in requesting that the parents have professionals (like a firefighter or a police officer) review each parent's restraints for proper installation.

B. Swimming Pools

Like child restraints, most states will have their own regulations about appropriate swimming pool barriers (fences, locks, or covers) and when they are required. Some homes with pools are not subject to the barrier requirements if the home was built prior to the regulations. If a parent questions whether a particular home is required to have a pool fence or barrier, a city office or a private attorney will need to be consulted. A parent may request that they will go beyond the minimum requirements for pool safety and that each parent's home will have specific safeguards with specific fence and alarm requirements. While each parent will be free to start the child in swim lessons when they feel it's appropriate, the parents would also be well-served to collaborate in scheduling the swim lessons so that each is assured the child is becoming familiar with water safety.

C. Trampolines and Other "Dangerous" Activities

Ideally, a Plan will address how the child can safely participate in certain activities or if certain activities will be avoided until a certain age. The Plan could address that the child will not use guns or attend gun safety classes until a certain age, and whether either parent has a trampoline at home or will allow the child to use a trampoline elsewhere. If a child is already involved in activities like horseback riding, motocross, or contact sports, that should be specified in the Plan along with any agreements the parents have about restrictions and use of safety equipment.

If one parent determines, without the agreement of the other, that a child can engage in activities that arguably have some element of danger, including trampolines, horseback riding, or the use of legal fireworks, it will be difficult for a family court to prohibit that otherwise legal activity. A parent who believes certain activities to be dangerous to a child must do their own research to learn what a given locality (where the other parent lives) prohibits and cannot presume that certain activities will be disallowed by the court. Parents have very different levels of tolerance for danger to a child. Just as one parent cannot force the other to allow a child to handle fireworks, it will be difficult for the more careful parent to prevent the less restrictive parent from having legal fireworks.

Some of the specified activities will have legal regulations that can be applied. A child's use of guns, whether for a specific hunting activity, target practice, or gun safety lessons, as well as the use of fireworks, are things possibly regulated in some areas. A parent who may disagree with the child's use of guns or fireworks while with the other parent should research what is legal for the child's age.

A final note about what the court might do in the case of a dangerous activity. A careful parent may believe that they can convince a judge (or a parenting coordinator or someone else with authority over the parenting relationship) that a certain given activity is too dangerous for the child. The person with authority will generally attempt, however, not to substitute personal opinions about an activity over the judgment of the parent. The concept of the fundamental right to a parent is important in the court system, and even a judge who has some authority over parenting will, in most cases, concede to a parent's individual judgment unless that judgment is demonstrably dangerous to the child or contrary to a specific law or regulation. Just as judges will not designate what a parent must feed a child or a child's specific bedtime. A child's activities can vary depending on what their parent believes is reasonably safe.

D. Child Walking to School

While a child resides with a parent, that parent is responsible for getting the child to and from school at proper times. (See School Tardies and Absences in Chapter 9.) A parent may use their own personal judgment to decide that a child is capable of walking or riding their bike to school on their own. In general, that decision will belong to the residential parent and is not usually covered by regulations.

E. Motorcycles and Off-Road Motorized Vehicles

Parents should discuss and attempt to agree on what, if any, motorized vehicles (bikes, minibikes, scooters, mopeds, etc.) will be permitted for a child, at what age, and under what restrictions. A child may already be using some vehicles at the time of the parents' separation, so use of the parameters they used while together would be helpful. In some families, riding off-road vehicles like dune buggies or sand buggies is a part of most family celebrations, so recognition of what the child is used to is important. In the case of disagreement between parents, some jurisdictions may have regulations that cover a child's use of a motorcycle or off-road motorized vehicles, and those regulations should be followed. Some regulations on these items may apply to smaller jurisdictions (cities and communities) rather than statewide, so research is necessary to find out exactly what is and is not permitted in a particular small area. A prohibition of certain motorized vehicles may be in effect for children under age 14, with some requirement of consent form for children age 14 and over, again dependent on jurisdiction.

Research should include what helmet or safety equipment requirements are in effect, such as closed-toed leather footwear, and at a minimum, the Plan should provide for what safety gear will be required for the activities.

A parent who objects to a child's use of these vehicles while at the other parent's home should be prepared to do their own research about what is prohibited in a certain area and should not presume that a child's use of motorized vehicles is automatically prohibited. If a child's use of these vehicles is technically permitted under a locality's regulations, it is doubtful a family court will stop a parent from allowing what is technically legal.

F. Child as Babysitter

Ideally, a Plan will provide when an older sibling may presumptively take care of younger siblings at home or when an only child can start staying at home on their own. Co-parents can discuss the issue with each other and with the child to determine the child's level of comfort and interest in staying home alone or acting as a babysitter for younger children.

The issue may first arise for an only child and when that child is old enough and mature enough to stay home on their own without a caretaker.

It will be rare to find a specific age designated when either staying home alone, or acting as a babysitter, is absolutely safe. Most states do not have laws specifying at what age a child can be left unsupervised.

There are many factors to be considered by one or both parents in making these decisions, and one of the most important would be, for what limited period of time, during daylight hours, should staying alone at home begin? Few parents would dispute that the gradual testing of a child's independence should start with the child staying home for a few minutes or a couple of hours, during daylight hours, while a parent is nearby running errands.

Other important factors to address will be:

- Does the child know how to reach the parent?

- How far away is the parent?

- Does the child have a cell phone?

- What is the child's feeling about staying alone for that period of time?

- Does the child know how to get emergency help/call 911 (or the emergency number in that country)?

- Is there a neighbor nearby to go to or who can check in on the child?

- How is the absent parent checking in on the child, and how often?

- How safe is the home, and is there a properly barriered pool?

- What are the ages of younger siblings, if any?

Careful consideration of these factors, combined with the child's maturity, will lead some parents to feel comfortable leaving the child (either alone or with younger children), starting with short periods of time and perhaps daylight hours only. If a child is showing fear or reluctance to staying home alone, the issue should not be forced.

The American Red Cross and other organizations offer babysitting classes, most of which start for children in grades 6-8 and above, which gives an approximate age parameter for consideration of when a child may babysit.

Most importantly, if the parents disagree with when a child is ready to be home alone, the parent who is allowing this to happen should share their analysis of the factors listed above with the other parent, to show that this issue was carefully thought out before the child is left home alone.

Unfortunately, it is sometimes the case that the child expresses to Parent A that they do not feel comfortable when Parent B leaves them alone at home. This puts Parent A in a difficult position as the child may be expressing to Parent B that they are fine with the situation. This situation may require the input of a counselor or child interviewer to establish the child's feelings so that Parent A is not accused of merely expressing their own feelings on the subject.

If police or government child services are called to the home to check on the child (called by either the other parent or a concerned neighbor or family member), an assessment of risk to the child will be done, and the absent parent may be contacted by police. Every parent must use their best judgment in determining safety issues to avoid the possibility of outside interventions to protect the child's safety.

G. Unsafe Pets

In crafting an effective Parenting Plan where the child may be in the presence of an animal that a parent believes may be unsafe (such as a biting dog), the primary concern should be the safety of the child. If a pet has been shown to be unsafe or unfamiliar with children, safety measures should be implemented, including secure confinement of the animal in a designated area when the child is present. Evidence of regular veterinary check-ups and behavioral assessments may also be shared with the objecting parent to show ongoing monitoring of the animal's temperament. In cases where the animal risk remains unmitigated, the Parenting Plan may necessitate supervised visitation until the pet concerns are addressed. The goal is to strike a balance between maintaining a child-friendly environment and addressing the unique challenges posed by the presence of a potentially dangerous animal in the household.

H. Covid and the Pandemic

Entire books have been written about parental judgment and appropriate Covid-related measures for a child. Countless parents have engaged in disagreements about masking, being in public places, attending school and activities, traveling, and other concerns and measures related to potential Covid transmission for children.

Suggested Covid and related issues of health concern could be covered in Plan clauses like:

In the event of a pandemic or national health emergency, as established by the United States CDC or national or local health organizations, we agree to continue to abide by our Parenting Plan provisions and parenting schedule to the extent reasonably possible in light of restrictions. Should it appear that exchanges of child cannot reasonably take place due to government restrictions, we agree to provide the parent who does not have child with frequent (at least daily) Facetime or video contact, and we agree to closely monitor all available updates which would allow a return to the parenting schedule.

We agree that when recommended by the CDC or required by child's school district or activities, we will engage in masking while in public and will provide child with medical masks and follow any other recommended protocols.

For all testing done in either of our households, the test results will be exchanged between us as soon as obtained, including testing of child. We agree that we will each exercise our independent judgment when child is in our care as to when to have child tested, but if either parent is kept away from child for a period in excess of seven days due to travel or other restrictions, the parent who has child will, upon request, have child tested within a reasonable amount of time.

We agree that we will each exercise our independent judgment in when to send child to school or other activities during such an emergency.

In those cases where a governmental agency has issued regulations relating to pandemic procedures, a family court can enforce those regulations and will likely rule on the side of a parent who is in favor of those regulations against a parent who violates them. If a school district has put a mask mandate into effect, a family court will likely enforce that mandate against a violating parent. Similarly, if a mask mandate is not formally in effect in each area, a parent attempting to force masking on the other parent's household (for either the child or the entire household) will likely lose, as masking, in that case, is left to individual judgment.

Following mask mandates, which are in effect for airports and other types of transportation, will be considered to be in the child's best interests, and a parent who determines to violate that type of federal regulation with the child is likely to be sanctioned by a family court. The issue is not one of whether the masking is appropriate or not in a given situation but a parent's compliance with governmental rules; noncompliance with governmental rules will likely be considered to be an assumption of risk or harm to the child. (See Vaccinations in Chapter 7.)

CHAPTER 9

Educational Decisions

Education is a major issue for co-parents of any school-age child. In drafting your Parenting Plan, you'll want to be sure you are adequately covering matters related to education. In particular:

- The Plan should list the name of where the child attends school now, and whether either parent has the right to decide on a change of school. If the child has not yet started kindergarten, the choice of kindergarten should be designated if possible. If a specific school can't be designated, even a statement about what school district or area of the community will be utilized and will assist with the school decision later.

- The Plan should designate whether the parents have agreed to utilize one childcare facility or whether each parent will choose their own childcare facility to use during their own parenting time.

- A procedure for choosing a school should be outlined to say what happens when the child can no longer attend their current school because they graduate or need to leave the school for another reason.

- The Plan should outline how it will be determined if the child requires academic assistance and support, including tutoring.

- The Plan should state who has the right to sign consents relating to the child's academic education. In general, if the parents have joint decision-making authority, they will both need to sign for major decisions. But if the consent is for a single-day activity like a field trip, the parent who has residential custody of the child on that day should be in charge of required consents. If the consent is for testing, inoculation, or an invasive procedure, that decision likely requires joint approval of the parents as this would not be a one-day (or day-to-day) decision.

The specific areas below are important to discuss between parents and included in a Parenting Plan. The goal in dealing with these issues proactively is to ensure no disruption in the child's education and no uncertainty for a child about where they will be attending school.

A. School Enrollment and Decisions

Parents sometimes can't agree on what school a child is to attend. If the parents' disagreement comes after a child is already established in a school, most courts would favor the *status quo*, meaning the child is likely to stay in the current school absent significant evidence that that school is objectively bad for them, and not just that another school might be somewhat better.

Sometimes there is no *status quo* school, if the child is just starting kindergarten, or is finishing up at a certain school (such as 8th grade graduation). In those cases, a school needs to be chosen for the first time.

The parents may also have legitimate differences of opinion about what school offers the best environment for the child's educational, physical, and emotional needs. For older children (starting high school), there may be considerations such as activities and enrichment offered by a particular school where the child's friends will be attending. The child's wishes should be considered in the school selection.

Too often, a parents' choice of school will center on convenience to the parent's home or how easy it is to get the child to and from school or the school hours that are most convenient to the parent's schedule. (See One Parent's Desire to Change Schools later in this chapter.)

When the parents can't agree on a choice of school after significant discussion and exchange of all information and options, the school choice may be left up to the courts. In making that decision, the court will consider many factors, such as the child's needs and the various schools, and whether a change of school is necessary at all. Some factors to be considered are whether the school has academic and non-academic (extracurriculars) for the child; whether the child has special needs (physical or educational) and how those needs can be met at each potential school; and the child's academic and disciplinary history at school.

B. Access to School Information and Homework

Unless there are specific court orders stating that a parent may not have access to this information, both parents are presumptively entitled to school information about their children. This means a school should communicate (in a reasonable way) with both parents. A school may require proof of the parent's identity and copies of court orders to determine with whom the school needs to communicate. Each parent should be entitled to information about how to log into a school's portal to see the child's grades and attendance history. Schools should hopefully give each parent a separate username and password so the parents can log in separately. It's important to note that each parent has a responsibility to keep themselves informed about the child's school information. It's not reasonable to expect one parent to educate the other about the child's school calendar, grades, and other school-related activities that are found on the school website.

Potential language for school information clauses include:

Each parent will have access to the child's educational and related records directly from the school, including access to any online school portals. Each parent is expected to keep themselves familiar with all school records and to regularly consult the school portal and school calendar. Neither parent has the responsibility to keep the other parent notified of school activities. When a parent receives notification from the school about a last-minute change or has reason to believe that the other parent has not received notice of a particular school event or activity, the parent receiving notice will forward that notice to the other parent.

Each parent is responsible for seeing that the child completes homework, reading, take-home activities, and other types of schoolwork during that parent's parenting time. The parents will keep each other reasonably notified of the status of multi-day schoolwork and projects.

Where necessary, when a very young child brings home a weekly folder of schoolwork or has regular activities, this additional provision may be necessary.

Both parents agree to maintain a dedicated folder for the child containing essential school homework, notices, and school communications, as well as extracurricular activity notices and schedules. This folder will be exchanged between the parents.

The folder, which travels with the child from school, will be reviewed and updated by the parent who receives the child on folder day. Each parent is responsible for adding any new documents and ensuring that all relevant information is current and accurate and forwarded to the other parent upon the child's exchange. During each custody exchange, the folder shall be handed over to the receiving parent.

In the event of any loss or damage to the folder or its contents, the parent responsible shall notify the other parent immediately and take steps to replace the necessary documents.

C. Kindergarten and Elementary School

Parents naturally want to be informed of everything that's going on with their child's education, particularly their early education and grade school years. When children are very young, their schoolwork may be sent home in a weekly take-home folder instead of posted online. The weekly folder can be problematic if sent home, for example, every Wednesday, because that means only one parent is receiving the folder and information, and that information is not readily available to the other parent. If the weekly send-home folder routine is in effect in your child's school, the parent receiving the folder has the responsibility to provide information to the other parent. This can be done by copying or scanning everything in the folder to the other parent weekly. The parent receiving the information can also review all information, make copies or scans of the information to keep, then pass the folder on to the other parent at the next exchange.

Time-sensitive material such as the weekly spelling words or immediate assignments should be immediately copied, scanned or photographed for the other parent so that type of work can be done at the other parent's home as soon as the child arrives there.

Ideally, the school portal will provide each parent with online information about homework, tests, and any missing projects. Parents need to communicate frequently and specifically to exchange information about projects and books. Projects, electronics, and materials may have to be transported between households. Sample parenting clauses to cover elementary school issues could be:

> Both parents shall have full access to the school's online parent portals (e.g., ClassDojo. Gradelink, PowerSchool, ParentVue, Google Classroom, etc.) to monitor and support the child's academic progress. If the school does not provide separate login accounts for each parent, the parents shall create a shared login ID and password. This shared login information shall not be changed, modified, or restricted without the express consent of both parents. Both parents are responsible for ensuring that they can access the portal and for notifying the other parent immediately if any access issues arise.

> The parents shall scan and share with the other parent by email the same day of receipt the following: all information in the child's homework folder, spelling words, and any other necessary educational materials.

The parents shall exchange the child's homework folder, spelling words, and any other necessary educational materials at the time of custody exchange by placing the same in the child's backpack.

When a child is in a parent's care, he/she shall ensure that the child's homework is completed, the child's school-issued computer is fully charged, and all necessary materials are packed for the school day. If any larger or multi-day projects are sent home while the child is with one parent, that parent shall notify the other parent and provide the necessary information for continuity in assisting the child.

D. Parent-Teacher Conferences

Parent-teacher conferences are always important, but perhaps more so in the very early grades. The parents need to decide if they will schedule and attend the conferences together or attempt to set up separate conferences. Some schools and teachers will accommodate separate conferences, but some simply don't have the time to schedule two conferences for one child. If the parents can't agree to attend an in-person conference together, they should explore doing a virtual (Zoom) conference where both parents appear virtually or have one parent attend in person and the other be available by telephone. No matter how it's done, attending the same conference at the same time is preferable for all so that both parents receive the same information from the teacher at the same time to avoid any misinterpretations caused by one parent trying to pass on information. Proposed Plan language for school conferences could be:

Both parents have the right to attend parent-teacher conferences. The parents should endeavor to attend conferences together, either in person or with one or both parents attending online or by telephone. The parents recognize that the school or teacher may not be able to offer separate conferences. Either parent may ask the school to hold separate conferences if necessary. If only one parent attends a school conference, that parent will forward all information from the conference by email to the other parent within 24 hours, including submission of any documents received at the conference.

E. Transition from Middle School to High School

As a child enters middle school (sometimes called junior high school, and usually including 7th and 8th grades), decisions need to be made about where they will attend high school. Some middle schools naturally flow into a particular high school, with a high percentage of the middle school students all moving on to the same high school. Other middle schools will be more diversified and may feed into several high schools. High schools often have special strengths, including an emphasis on STEM, cultural activities (band, music, art, theater, orchestra), or a concentration on college preparation. By this age, the child may have preferences for what high school to attend, and the child's wishes should be sought in the most appropriate way. (See Child Interviews in Chapter 5.)

F. One Parent's Desire to Change Schools

Even after a child is attending school, and before a school transition is made necessary by a grade change, one parent may want to change the school. The reasons for wanting a change are numerous: a parent may feel the school isn't meeting the child's needs, is too easy or too difficult for the child, or the child may be bullied, have disciplinary problems, or feel the teachers don't like them. Social considerations such as lack of friends or even bullying may come into play. One of the most common reasons for a parent to want a change of school is the driving distance from a parent's home to the school. Jurisdictions will vary in how a court will consider a proposed change of school, but it's likely that the parent who wants to change the school will have the burden of proof and must show a good reason for the change. Most courts would not consider a major change of school without substantial evidence that the new school will be more beneficial for the child (and not just for the parent). This is one area where the status quo and preservation of the child's current situation will be favored. This is a dispute in which it may be helpful to engage a parenting coordinator as they are regularly tasked with selecting a child's school when the parents cannot agree upon the school.

G. Parents Living a Substantial Distance Apart

Divorce and separation cause many changes for children, and one major change is that each parent needs to find a separate place to live. A parent's relocation depends on finances, personal preferences, work location, types of transportation available, and whether the parent moves in with a new partner or family.

One parent may consider the location of the child's school to be the most important factor in choosing a new residence, while the other parent may not care how far the new home is from school.

In larger metropolitan areas, it's not unusual to find parents who technically live in the same city but have driving time of an hour or more between their homes. When the parents live that far apart and choosing a school is necessary, it's common for each parent to promote a school close to their house. Some parents propose as a compromise that a school be chosen that is equidistant from each home. If considering a mid-point school, consider the effect on the child of going to school that is far from both homes, potentially putting them far away from friends no matter which home they are at.

Parents need to seriously consider the commute to school when choosing where to live. A parent who voluntarily moves a great distance away from a child's established school will likely find little sympathy for the long drive they have voluntarily taken on.

If the parents live a substantial distance apart at the time the Plan is created, they will need to deal with the distance issues in the Plan by stating where the child will attend school. But the distance issue is one that often comes up several years after the Plan is created, as people move, take different jobs, and re-partner. A provision in the Plan that states:

"Unless the parents mutually agree otherwise, the child will presumptively remain in the current school district XXXX despite the relocation of either or both parents."

This is a good idea to prevent relocations from creating school conflict.

H. Parenting Time and Presence at School

Parents sometimes feel that even when it's not their assigned parenting time, they can visit the child's school to see the child during the school day. Schools often frown on uninvited parent visits to school. Even if the school has not objected to a parent coming to school unannounced, the CP may feel it inappropriate if the other parent is interrupting the school day (or lunch hour) to have additional time with the child. Most parents can work this situation out without intervention, but in some cases, specific restrictions on coming to school during the school day and during the other parent's parenting time are necessary. Clauses like the following can be implemented in severe cases:

A.   *Parents' Involvement on School Days: Father may assist or visit the child at their school (including having lunch with them) on his parenting days, which are Mondays, Tuesdays and Fridays; Mother may assist or visit the child at school (including having lunch with them) on her parenting days which are Wednesdays, Thursdays and Fridays. Each parent is presumptively entitled to volunteer at school, including volunteering for field trips, on their assigned parenting days.*

B.   *When it is the other parent's assigned parenting day, the NCP is not to visit the school (including having lunch there) or undertake other activities at school that involve volunteering other than the exceptions stated herein.*

C.   *Neither parent will attend the child's lessons, practices, or activities on the other parent's parenting day, other than any specifically defined activities listed below.*

D.   *Either parent may continue to visit the school or activities during the other parent's parenting time for the following: parties or events at school (such as a holiday program or recital or the type of party where all parents are invited); a parent bringing a forgotten item to a child, at the request of the custodial parent or teacher; a parent handling an administrative matter such as dropping off forms or payments to a school or administrative office (with no attempt to visit the child); a game or tournament for a sports activity.*

The above clause also covers a situation where the parents cannot agree who may accompany the child or the child's class on a field trip. Generally, the field trip priority should go with the parent who has scheduled parenting time that day, and if that parent chooses not to attend the field trip, they should notify the other parent to allow the NCP to try to attend. Sample clauses addressing field trips might be:

The parents shall alternate volunteer opportunities for field trips so that each parent has an opportunity to attend a field trip with the child.

or

When the child or parent receives notice of a field trip by way of a class note, posting, portal announcement, or permission slip, the other parent shall be notified of the date, time, and location of the field trip within one day of the notice.

Unless otherwise agreed in writing between the parties, only one parent shall be permitted to attend the child's field trips as a chaperone. Significant others are not permitted to attend absent agreement by the parents.

The parent with parenting time the day of the planned field trip has the first right of attendance as a chaperone. They shall indicate in writing to the other parent whether they will or will not attend the child's field trip as a chaperone. This message shall be provided by the parent with parenting time on the day of the field trip at least 14 days prior to the start of the field trip. If a parent elects not to attend the field trip, the other parent is permitted to attend. The other parent should provide notice of their intent to chaperone after receipt of the message from the parent with the first right of refusal. Unless agreed in writing, the parties shall not change their decision to attend later. If the parent with parenting time on the day of the field trip fails to provide timely notice under this provision (at least 14 days), that parent shall not be permitted to attend and has waived their right to chaperone the field trip in question. The other parent may attend and should provide an email indicating that intention as soon as possible after the 14-day period above.

I. Testing

Various types of testing, evaluations, and/or assessments are available through schools. Parents may be given the opportunity (or may request) to have their child tested for gifted status, ADD, other learning disabilities, hearing, eyesight, or other conditions. If the parents don't agree on testing, it's often necessary to name a neutral third party to be a tiebreaker about whether certain testing or evaluations should be done. Educational consultants (usually a mental health professional or school psychologist) are available to assist the parents in discussing these decisions and mediating a conclusion. If the parents can't agree on ADD or other learning disability assessments through the school, they may consider testing through a private institution or private psychologist who will take input from both parents, teachers, and the child.

J. Notice of Education Issues

Parents may receive difficult communications from the school. If a parent receives notice of disciplinary issues, problems, injuries, poor grades, missing assignments, and other "bad news" issues, immediate notice must be given to the other parent. The parent receiving the information should immediately respond to the school (or teacher) and include the other parent's contact information, with a request that the other parent be simultaneously included in all communications. Schools generally do know that both parents should be simultaneously contacted, but even the best of schools and teachers will occasionally make mistakes and contact only one parent. If a parent continually communicates with a school or teacher without bringing in the other parent, that can be a serious violation of co-parenting orders.

Each parent is individually responsible for being familiar with the school calendar. As stated earlier, each parent is expected to keep themselves informed about school schedules. School calendars are either publicly available online or are provided to parents through personalized online portals and it is each parent's responsibility to get entry into the school portal. Neither parent is responsible for reminding the other about no-school days, early release days, or special activities that are clearly posted on the official school calendar.

The Plan clause language stated earlier in this chapter about access to school information and parent-teacher conferences should adequately address notices received from the school.

Every state requires some amount of advance notice to be given to a child's parents before a 504 Plan or an Individualized Education Plan (IEP) evaluation or meeting. When it comes to these meetings, many individuals are often present, including teachers, administrators, the school social worker, and the school psychologist. These meetings are substantive, difficult to schedule, and hard to duplicate for separated parents. Therefore, parents should make every effort to notify each other of any 504 or IEP meetings, even beyond the standard notification requirements in the Parenting Plan. If possible, parents should attempt to attend these meetings together. Virtual meetings, when permitted, may serve as an acceptable alternative to in-person meetings.

If your child is on an IEP or 504, a provision as follows may be helpful to include in a Parenting Plan:

> *In the event either parent is notified of any meeting and/or change related to the child's IEP or 504 Plan, that parent shall send the other parent a copy of the notice within 24 hours of receipt. Both parties shall prioritize these meetings in their schedule to the extent possible and attend these meetings together.*

K. School Absences and Tardies

A parent may, during their own parenting time, determine to keep a child home from school or to allow the child to go in late or leave early. When this becomes excessive, the parents may have conflict about when a child may be taken out of school for anything other than a true illness.

Some parents believe it is acceptable for a child to miss school to accommodate vacation travel, to do family special days, or see relatives who are visiting. Other parents feel a child should not miss any school for personal reasons. Schools have an interest in a child's good attendance and will send home letters of concern if a child has excessive absences in a semester. Most jurisdictions have truancy laws about the number of days in a semester or school year that a child must attend. As an example, Arizona's truancy law at this writing is:

15-803. *School attendance; exemptions; definitions*

A. It is unlawful for any child who is between six and sixteen years of age to fail to attend school during the hours school is in session unless either:

1. The child is excused.

2. The child is accompanied by a parent or a person authorized by a parent.

3. The child is provided with instruction in a homeschool.

B. A child who is habitually truant or who has excessive absences may be adjudicated an incorrigible child as defined in section 8-201. Absences may be considered excessive when the number of absent days exceed ten percent of the number of required attendance days prescribed in section 15-802, subsection B, paragraph 1.

C. For the purposes of this section:

1. "Habitually truant" means a child who is truant for at least five school days within a school year.

2. "Truant" means an unexcused absence for at least one class period during the day.

3. "Truant child" means a child who is between six and sixteen years of age and who is not in attendance at a public or private school during the hours that school is in session unless excused as provided by this section.

In this case, Arizona law has designated either the "ten percent of school days" or "five days per school year" as a presumption that a child is missing too much school. If the other parent objects to a child's repeated absences that are not based on the child's illness, the statutory definition of excessive absences may come into play.

The same criteria come into play if a child is chronically late to school or is repeatedly taken out of school early by a parent. A modification of parenting time may be called for if one parent cannot get a child to school on time or repeatedly takes the child out of school early for convenience.

A sample clause to cover this type of situation, should it become a problem in your case, could be:

Each parent is responsible for determining if the child is too ill to attend school on their parenting time days, and that determination of illness will not be unreasonably questioned by the other parent. When a parent has determined that the child will stay home sick from school (or will be arriving at school late or picked up early for illness), that parent will notify the other parent immediately by email, including specifics of the illness and whether the child will be taken to the doctor or Urgent Care.

Neither parent may cause child to miss school, either for a full day, a late start, or an early release, for any reason except an illness as noted above or an absence due to a necessary medical provider appointment. Documentation of the medical provider appointment will be made to the other parent by email before school (or any part of a school day) is missed. If a parent wishes to take a child out of school for personal reasons, including travel, a special event, or seeing a family member, permission from the other parent will be obtained in advance. The parent who is keeping the child out of school is responsible for notifying the school and obtaining teacher approval for the absence, including obtaining makeup work for the child.

Consider both sides:

Nicole: Within reason, parents should be able to take the child out of school early or allow the child to miss school for an important event or vacation. Time with the family and these special trips are important, and one missed day will not make a difference in the child's academic performance.

Annette: The child's academic or social development may be negatively affected when a parent takes a child out of school or keeps them home from school without a good reason. Doing these things may tell the child that school is not important and doing so without the permission of the other parent and the school (individual teachers) shows a disregard for education and could result in the child's grades falling.

If parents cannot agree on whether to take a child out of school for a non-mandatory event, strict limitations on each parent's ability to take a child out of school (as shown in the suggested language above) may be implemented and are probably appropriate to avoid excessive absences.

L. EXCEPTIONAL CHILDREN

The Child with a Disability

In this book, we will use the term "child with a disability" to refer to a child with one or multiple physical, mental, intellectual, and/or developmental impairments. The limitations created by the disability can be mild to severe and affect a child's ability to move, communicate, learn, or engage socially. The following are a few examples of disabilities that may impair a child: Autism Spectrum Disorder, Cerebral Palsy, Down Syndrome, Muscular Dystrophy, Multiple Sclerosis (MS), Parkinson's Disease, deafness, blindness, orthopedic impairments, health impairments such as childhood leukemia or cancer, epilepsy, or diabetes, learning disabilities such as Attention-Deficit/Hyperactivity Disorder (ADHD), traumatic brain injury, and visual or speech/language impairments.

There are many different types of disabilities, and it is difficult to provide sample language for a Parenting Plan that would address each child's individual needs. Generally, parents of a child with a disability should consider additional Parenting Plan provisions to address how decisions are made, how care is implemented, and how disputes are resolved regarding the child's educational plan, therapies, medical/psychological providers, expenses related to the child, and long-term planning for the child.

A child with developmental needs may receive government benefits and the family may qualify for respite care. Court orders need to be clear as to how the parents share in the benefits and the respite care. In general, the parents should share in benefits including respite care in proportion to their parenting time and responsibilities for the child.

A child with a disability may have many special appointments or meetings including those for evaluation, specialists, therapies, etc. that parents should consider addressing in their Parenting Plan. For example, a Parenting Plan for a child with a speech delay could include who will schedule and transport the child to weekly speech therapy appointments. The parents should consider how they will schedule, give notice of, accommodate, and attend appointments. The use of a central calendar as discussed in Chapter 5 will be helpful.

In some cases, it makes sense for one parent to be primarily tasked with making appointments, as trying to share responsibility for such extensive scheduling will result in things being missed or duplicated. The parent making the appointments and doing the scheduling should place all appointments on the shared calendar for the other parent. As much as possible, therapy sessions that occur in the home, such as speech, occupational, Applied Behavioral Analysis (ABA) therapy, or physical therapy, should occur in each parent's home in proportion to each parent's scheduled time with the child.

In addition, both parents may need to follow certain recommended interventions or protocols for managing and supporting the child. If you believe a parent may not implement these interventions or follow recommendations in their own home, it may be helpful to insert a provision into the Parenting Plan addressing these concerns. An example of a provision addressing care of a child on the Autism Spectrum and recommendations from the child's occupational therapist might look like this:

The parties understand that the child's occupational therapist (OT) may implement specific strategies and techniques as they work with the child, which are aimed at improving daily living skills, enhancing sensory processing, and fostering social interaction and communication. The parties agree each will be separately trained by the OT in the necessary intervention or strategy, and each will follow the OT's recommendation when caring for the child.

If you are co-parenting a child with a disability, you and the other parent must first acknowledge the unique needs of the child and then find a way to support that child. This may be harder than it appears, as parents can disagree on the child's diagnosis and effective treatment and services.

Autism Spectrum Disorder is one example of a disability that can be the source of great conflict between co-parents. This is because parents may disagree as to whether the child is on the spectrum due to personal, professional, and ideological reasons. In addition, disputes may arise regarding treatment approaches. This is complicated by the spread of misinformation and pseudoscience around autism. While an entire book could be written regarding the complex interplay of differing beliefs about the nature and treatment of autism spectrum disorder, the take-away is that parents should rely on the diagnosis and advice of licensed professionals who are well-respected in their field and who have expertise in developmental disorders. These include developmental pediatricians, licensed child psychologists and psychiatrists, speech/language pathologists, behavior analysts, and occupational therapists. These do not include life coaches, celebrities, or websites that espouse false information based solely on opinion or anecdotal evidence.

An example of a decision-making provision for a child with an Autism Spectrum Disorder diagnosis is as follows:

The parties acknowledge that the child has been diagnosed with Autism Spectrum Disorder (ASD) by Dr. Smith. The parties agree to communicate and attempt to agree on all treatment and care provisions that arise for the child due to this diagnosis. The parties understand that disagreements may arise as to the treatment and care of the child. In the event the parties are unable to agree on a course of treatment or care provider for the child, the parties shall rely upon and follow the recommendation of Dr. Smith as long as that recommendation is made in writing to both parties.

When it comes to the education of a child with a disability, they may be on an Individualized Education Plan (IEP) or a 504 Plan. These are blueprints for how a child with a qualifying disability will have access to learning at their school. They provide services and changes to meet a child's needs at school. The rules for IEPs as opposed to 504 Plans are slightly different. An IEP results in curriculum changes and special education. Section 504 Plans do not result in a curriculum change, instead accommodations are made for the child within the typical curriculum.

Note that children in private or charter schools may obtain support through IEPs/504s, but the process and extent of services provided can differ from those in public schools. While public school districts are required to offer a Free Appropriate Public Education (FAPE) to children with disabilities, this obligation does not extend fully to private school students. Instead, the district may provide some services through an Individual Service Plan (ISP). District school psychologists will do evaluations at private schools. Charter schools are public in that they must provide an evaluation and receive funds to provide services. Sometimes, when services are appropriate, they may have to occur at a public school.

A 504 Plan does not necessarily require a psychoeducational evaluation. A letter from the child's pediatrician may suffice to meet eligibility requirements. As it relates to IEPs, a child can be referred for a psychoeducational evaluation by a teacher, doctor, or other professional. Parents can make the referral by writing a formal request to the school's special education department, which will trigger a meeting with school stakeholders to discuss their concerns. Before an evaluation can begin, parents will need to give informed consent. Generally, parents should agree to the evaluation or agree to obtain a private evaluation from a professional they both agree on. The information from the evaluation will be useful to parents in supporting their child. If the evaluation indicates the child meets the criteria for an IEP or a 504 Plan, the school will create a team of teachers, administrators, and psychologists to address what accommodations and services will best serve the child's disability. Parents are active and required members of this team, and both parents should prioritize meetings related to a 504 Plan or IEP in their schedule. IEP meetings must be held every year, and 504 Plans are updated annually. The appropriate services and accommodations are usually the source of higher conflict between parents as compared to obtaining the evaluation itself. Again, the best way to resolve these types of conflicts is to agree to a trained professional who will make the decision in the event of a dispute.

If you believe your child may qualify for an IEP or 504 Plan or your child is already on an IEP or 504 Plan, the following provisions may be helpful in addressing consent for evaluation and disputes regarding services and accommodations:

> If the child is suspected of having a disability and the child is referred for an evaluation by a teacher, doctor, psychologist, therapist, or other treating professional, both parents shall timely provide consent for this evaluation. Both parents shall also receive the results of this evaluation in writing.

> If a child qualifies for an IEP or 504 Plan, both parents shall immediately notify the other of the date/time of these meetings. Both parents shall engage in the meetings associated with either Plan. Both parents shall prioritize these meetings over other obligations and attend, if possible. Neither parent will unreasonably delay these meetings.

> The parents shall attempt to resolve any disputes that arise in the context of the child's IEP or 504 Plan. If they cannot, the parent shall rely upon the opinion of the school's psychologist or other treating professional as to the appropriate accommodation/support for the child.

The Gifted Child

You may be surprised to learn that gifted children are entitled to certain services under federal law, and testing is required for a child to be identified as "gifted."

Many schools use the results of an IQ and/or achievement test, such as the Naglieri General Ability Test (NAGC) or the Cognitive Abilities Test (CogAT), to assess whether a child is gifted or exceptional, although some schools will consider qualitative teacher and parent assessments. Schools offer these tests in a group setting a few times each year, or families may obtain private individual testing from a qualified psychologist.

If it is determined that a child is gifted per the district or school's criteria, the child may be invited to participate in a gifted or talented school, a development program, a cluster classroom, and/or a special class at their school. Gifted programming offers numerous benefits for children, including intellectual challenges, individualized learning, social-emotional support, increased motivation, and higher academic achievement.

Generally, if it is recommended that a child be tested for gifted eligibility, testing should happen. This information is important to parenting the child and meeting their needs. Conflict between co-parents is more likely to occur when co-parents address how to proceed after receiving the results of gifted testing.

Understanding the available gifted services in your school or district and their benefits is essential before making decisions with your co-parent regarding a gifted child. In addition to the school or district websites, there are many reputable sources and groups that provide helpful information about gifted children. One example is the National Association for Gifted Children (https://nagc.org/).

If a child has been identified as gifted, they are best served when parents jointly engage with and rely upon professionals regarding the child's gifted status. These professionals include psychologists, therapists, educational advocates or consultants, teachers, and school professionals. The goal in this engagement is to ensure both parents receive the same information and that everyone's concerns are equally addressed.

Note of Caution: While a gifted child may present as more "mature" or "adult," they may have the same level of emotional maturity and decision-making skills as other children their age.

The following provision may be helpful in addressing gifted testing and placement in a Parenting Plan:

If recommended by a professional at a child's school or a mental health professional treating the child, the parties shall consent for the child to undergo gifted testing as offered by the school or district. Both parents shall receive the results of the testing. If the child qualifies for one or more gifted accommodations, the parents shall discuss the available options and services for the child jointly. If the parents cannot agree on an appropriate solution, they shall rely upon the advice of the child's psychologist to resolve disputes and request any opinions from the psychologist in writing. Parents should avoid substantive verbal discussions with the psychologist outside of the other parent's presence.

CHAPTER 10

Extracurricular Decisions

What activities will the child be involved in, when, and who pays? Extracurriculars are a huge area for disputes between co-parents. While there's possibly of no right answer to the issue of extracurriculars, a child's involvement in extracurriculars is usually considered essential to help them master skills, socialize with peers, and find out their own real strengths and interests. Extracurriculars can either be a valuable growth opportunity for a child or, if the parents have disputes about the activity, extracurriculars can be a horrible experience.

When parents disagree about extracurriculars for a child, the objections generally fall into broad categories:

1. The parent who disagrees with the activity doesn't want to give up any of their parenting time. A subset of this reason is that the parent who disagrees doesn't want the responsibility for getting the child to the activity due to either loss of parenting time or just not wanting to make the drive.

2. The parent who disagrees with the activity genuinely doesn't believe the activity to be best for the child, and possibly promotes a different activity. A subset of this reason is that a child may be telling the parent they don't like the activity.

3. A parent disagrees with the activity because the other parent (or the other parent's partner) is intimately involved with the activity as a coach or participant.

4. A parent doesn't want to be financially responsible for the activity.

Not every state (or jurisdiction) has a statute or rule regarding extracurricular activities and expenses for these activities. You'll need to come to your own agreements and include them in your Parenting Plan. By addressing these issues carefully in your Plan, you can minimize friction.

Let's take a closer look at each of these issues.

A. Concerns about Parenting Time

In most joint legal decision-making situations, the decisions about extracurricular activities will allow each parent to make decisions for their own parenting time and will be stated something like this:

Neither parent will sign up or register a child for an extracurricular activity which meets or practices during, or otherwise affects the other parent's parenting time, unless the other parent has agreed to the activity in advance.

In other words, if the parents have a 5/2/2/5 schedule, neither parent could enroll the child in an activity that meets every Friday or every weekend because those times alternate between the parents every week. But in a 5/2/2/5 schedule, a parent could enroll a child in a dance class that meets every Tuesday, as long as that parent is the Tuesday parent. A Tuesday lesson or activity would not interfere with the other parent's parenting time.

Especially as a child ages, once-a-week lessons or activities are less common and less available. Participation in sports, particularly team sports, usually involves a schedule of two or more practices a week, plus additional practices and games on weekends. Tournaments or meet schedules further complicate matters, and participation in a formal league or "club" (something usually organized outside of a school and involving overnight travel to play other teams) may cause problems with a "normal" parenting time schedule. The parents must cooperate to a high level to make those activities work as a child gets older. By the time a child is in middle school, sports and other activity schedules may be occurring several times a week.

In general, the child simply won't be able to engage in activities that occur during both parents' parenting times unless the parents agree, and so in the cases of parent disagreement, the Plan language stated above is likely to be in effect.

B. Legitimate Disagreement about What Activity Is Best

Parents can have reasonable, valid disagreements about what activity a child can participate in or how many activities. Some parents are fine with a child's participation in baseball, football, and basketball, and they take into account that those activities overlap for a few weeks each year.

The solution for many parents is an agreement that a child will be involved in only one activity per "season," with one parent choosing the fall season activity and the other choosing the spring season activity:

The parents agree that Jason can be involved in sports and agree to limit his sports to one sport per season, with the seasons described as (a) fall season, which includes sports beginning in (approximately) July, August, or September and continuing through the fall holidays, (b) spring season, which includes sports beginning in (approximately) November, December, or January and continuing through the end of the school year. If the parents cannot otherwise agree, then Father will choose the fall sport, and Mother will choose the spring sport. Once the sport has been chosen for a particular season, both parents agree to support Jason's activity in that sport and to take him to all scheduled meetings, practices, training, and games. In the event a parent is unable to transport Jason to a scheduled activity, the other parent will be asked if they can transport to that activity in lieu of Jason missing it. The parents recognize that there will be occasions when Jason needs to miss a scheduled sport activity for reasonable family activities including breaks and holidays. In reaching this agreement for two sports activities per school year, the parents are also agreeing to equally share in the costs of the chosen activities, with each parent to pay 50% of the required costs, including equipment.

Hopefully, each parent will be choosing the activity in consultation with the child. The term "season" must be specifically defined in this type of agreement. A material part of this type of agreement is that each parent agrees to cooperate with the activity and agrees to transport the child to required practices, games, and tournaments, even if they didn't choose that activity.

Parents should also discuss what happens if the CP can't get the child to a certain activity. Parents have conflicts at work or for personal matters and may not be able to drive the child to each practice. If that happens, the other parent (assuming they are supporting the activity) should be prepared to offer driving help at least occasionally. Both parents should explore carpools and ridesharing with friends to help with driving.

Both parents should discuss that taking on a group activity, whether it be a team sport or a dance troupe, means taking on responsibility to the rest of the group, and when a child misses even one practice, it affects the entire group and puts the child in a bad position with teammates. Parents should discuss the consequences that a missed practice or game will have on their child and on the rest of the team. A coach can't be expected to allow a child to have a major position in the group if the child regularly misses practices. An activity that is meant to increase a child's self-esteem will have the opposite effect if the child's failure to participate puts the whole team at risk.

A parent who objects to extracurriculars on the theory that "he and I do activities together" should consider how the child's participation with other kids helps the child individuate and make friends.

A note about parents who don't want to allow participation in extra-curriculars:

Consider both positions:

Nicole: We both know that he wants to play this sport! How can you not agree to take him to practice every week during your time? You even kept him home on purpose when he felt fine. We should both be taking him to all practices and games during our own time — no exceptions. It's not fair to the child because he loves this sport but can't fully participate because of you!

Annette: I agree that sports are important, but I don't have equal parenting time – I have way less parenting time than you do, and you enrolled him in the sport on Tuesdays, which is my only weekday with him. And now you expect me to take him to practice every Tuesday, which cuts my limited time down by 3 hours every single week. That's not fair.

C. Agreement to an Activity; Notice and Information

Activities can be discussed in person if the parents are able, but specific information about an activity should be exchanged in writing. A Plan provision like this is encouraged:

EXTRACURRICULAR ACTIVITIES. Neither parent will sign up or register a child for an extracurricular activity that meets or practices during, or otherwise affects, the other parent's parenting time unless the other parent has agreed to the activity in advance. When a parent wants to propose an activity for a child, information about the activity will be emailed to the other parent for consideration. All available information will be provided, including websites or documentation that give information about the activity. The parent who is requested to give input on a suggested activity will respond within 48 hours.

This type of provision requires that specific information be exchanged. If Mother wants the child to enroll in dance, simply saying, "Marissa would like to try a dance class," isn't enough information. Mother should propose and provide the following:

- The specific dance troupe/group by name.

- Website for the activity.

- The day of the week and time of class(es), if known, and the duration of each class, and where the classes will occur.

- The name of the dance instructor (or at least the person in charge of the dance school or group), including email address.

- The program or class costs, including any ancillary costs like shoes, costumes, uniforms, or registration fees. Sometimes, this information will be on the group's website, or each parent should consult with the instructor to find out specifics.

With all this information, the other parent can make a reasoned decision about whether they can agree to the activity.

D. Who Attends the Activities

Generally, the CP should be able to attend routine practices and lessons because it's their parenting time. Unless the parents get along extraordinarily well, the NCP should not attend those routine practices and lessons, as they may attend during their own parenting time.

Special events in the activity, such as games, recitals, award ceremonies, and all-parent functions (like a parent meeting or dinner) should be open to both parents, regardless of whose parenting time is happening during the event.

Suggested language (and this language is applied to a week-on/week-off alternating weeks schedule) could be:

With certain exceptions as noted below, the parent who does not have Trevor at a given time (the noncustodial parent or NCP) will not be present at school or at Trevor's activities. Specifically, Father may be present at Trevor's school and activities during Father's weeks, and Mother may be present at Trevor's school and activities during Mother's weeks. As the parents have an alternating week schedule with exchanges on Fridays, each parent's week is defined as beginning with Trevor's drop-off at school on Fridays. Each parent may be present at Trevor's activities on their own parenting time, including practices, meetings, and parties.

Both parents may however be present at Alexander's activities such as games, recitals, tournaments, and special programs regardless of parenting time, as these are considered special circumstances where both parents are routinely invited. Only the custodial parent may attend Alexander's lessons, practices, and ordinary day-to-day activities.

A situation that arises for some parents is when one parent puts the child in an activity (during his own parenting time), and the other parent does not take the child to rehearsals or practices, refuses to pay anything towards the activity, and in general doesn't support it, but then, the nonparticipating parent then wants to attend some games. In those situations, even a nonparticipating and nonpaying parent should likely be allowed to attend the major or special events in the activity, including games and recitals. Who pays for the activity does not determine who gets to attend. The activity is about the child.

One of the most difficult situations is when either a parent or stepparent has stepped in as coach for a child's activities. That person acting as coach naturally feels they are entitled to attend all practices, trainings, and related team activities, regardless of parenting schedules. In that event, unless the parent/stepparent who is acting as coach has abused the privilege and taken advantage of the situation by trying to deprive the other parent of parenting time, they likely must be permitted to act as coach and attend events regardless of the parenting time schedule. The coaching parent will likely be permitted to be present at all team activities, regardless of parenting time. It would be unfortunate if the child needed to stop an activity because of parental disagreement about the coaching issue, but if this type of situation involves court intervention, it is perhaps better that the child become engaged in an activity where the parents (or stepparents) are not permitted to use the activity as means for conflict.

E. Payment for Activities

Note that an agreement for a child to participate in an activity doesn't always mean an agreement that the parents will split the costs of that activity unless payment provisions are specifically stated. If sufficient information isn't provided up front, a parent could say, "Yes, it's fine with me if Marissa attends dance classes," but that parent may have no intention of paying a portion of class fees or costumes. Failing to mention the costs of an activity will result in misunderstandings and disagreements.

Suggested language could include:

"The parents, in discussing any proposed activity for Jason, will specifically discuss how the activity and all related costs (uniforms, equipment, shoes, travel, coaching, or training costs) will be paid, and will confirm in writing if the costs are to be shared and in what proportion. Neither parent is to assume that consent to engage in an activity includes consent to pay for that activity unless specifically agreed." (See Reimbursements in Chapter 16.)

A child's extracurricular activities are usually beneficial and possibly even crucial for the child's social development. Those activities also cause significant extra work for parents who may already, as single parents, feel overwhelmed with work, child care, and driving the kids around. Even parents who are still together may have disagreements about extracurriculars or accuse each other of forgetting to schedule an important event. When the parents are separated, everyday frustrations felt by most parents can turn into accusations against the other parent.

CHAPTER 11

Child's Possessions

The issue of a child's possessions, whether and if those possessions go back and forth between households, is fraught with conflict. Parents may differ greatly in what personal possessions they provide for a child and what they believe the child should have access to. A few ground rules and guidelines for the child's possessions may help to resolve some of the disputes.

A. Electronics Including Phones

Children, as a rule, have many electronics starting at an early age. Even a toddler may have an electronic game they love and play with frequently or a specialized watch. By the time the child is in late elementary or middle school, electronics could include cell phones, iPads, laptops, video consoles, charging cables, headsets, controllers, Apple Watches, and other game consoles and paraphernalia.

As with schoolbooks, if it's affordable and if the parents have a history

of disagreement about personal items and are high-conflict, having dupli-
cates of all possible items is a good solution. Duplicate possessions help
the parents stay out of each other's way and limit communication needed
about those items. The cost of duplicating devices (i.e., two iPads) could
be far less than the legal fees involved in fighting about one iPad. Certainly, in the case of charging cords and some peripheral devices, the cost of
duplicating the items in both houses should be negligible.

The category "electronic devices" includes any kind of device given
to the child that includes tracking abilities, including an Apple Watch, Gizmo Watch, Pinwheel Phone or Watch, Fitbit, Gabb Phone or Watch, etc.,
or an AirTag. The GPS locator involved in these and other items can cause
issues for some parents, as the NCP has the ability to track the child's
specific location while they're with the CP. If a child is given a watch with
a tracker and is asked to take the watch to the other parent's home, the
receiving parent should be specifically told that the child has the watch
and what it is. An attempt to send a watch or any type of tracking device with a child to the other parent's home without notice to the other
parent could be considered stalking, with significant criminal charges. An
attempt to conceal a tracking device, such as an AirTag, in a child's toy is
particularly indicative of a stalking attempt. If the CP objects to the child
retaining a watch or other tracking device during their parenting time,
then the CP is probably going to be justified in taking possession of the
watch or item and holding it for return to the parent who bought it.

Sample language involving a child's electronic device could be:

> Neither parent will send the child to the other parent's home with
> any type of tracking or GPS-related device unless the other parent
> is specifically told of the device. Examples of these items include a
> child's cell phone, Gizmo, Apple watch, AirTag, or any device with a
> "Find Me" app enabled, or any type of GPS tracker (placed on either
> the child's person or in a personal property item).

AirTags do have a place in exchanging a child, as the placement of
an AirTag in a child's carry-on luggage while flying (especially as an unaccompanied minor) is a valuable tool for both parents to track the child

during travel. Placement in the child's carry-on or even placing in a child's favorite stuffy could make sense during travel, as long as both parents are aware of the device. The AirTag should be removed or disabled by the receiving parent upon the child's arrival, however, so that tracking is limited to the actual travel time.

B. The "Wubby"

The term "Wubby" is used here to apply to all the comfort items a child needs or is attached to. Usually, for a child under the age of 8 or so, the Wubby might be a stuffed animal or favorite blanket and is generally something the child needs with them in order to sleep or be comforted. It should go without saying that if a young child is very attached to a comfort item, that item should travel back and forth between the parents' households with the child. This is one example of a situation where the parents need to coordinate to have the item transferred somehow, if the child is exchanged through school or a childcare provider. Transfer options include fitting this item into a backpack (with the child instructed that it's not to leave the backpack during the school day), or having the parents do a separate transfer of personal items (the Wubby, clothing, electronics, etc.) by drop-off on each exchange day.

C. Clothing and Shoes

The exchange of (or failure to exchange) a child's clothing and footwear is a huge area of disagreement for parents. A parent often feels that the other parent is intentionally stealing or retaining clothing that they didn't purchase. In some cases, the parents exchange countless emails asking that certain items of clothing or footwear be "returned" to the purchasing parent. When dealing with disputes about a child's clothing or footwear, remember the following:

- The clothing is the child's, not a parent's. Once purchased for the child, the child should not feel they are restricted from taking their favorite clothing items to the other parent's home.

- Children lose clothing. Always check the school lost and found before accusing the other parent of having an item. Just because something's missing doesn't mean the other parent is withholding it.

- A child should not be subjected to carrying a suitcase or backpack full of clothing to school on exchange days. A child should have plenty of clothing, shoes, underwear, socks, and personal care items at each parent's house and should not be transporting day-to-day needs between houses. Carrying a backpack of clothing makes a child feel like a homeless nomad or that they don't have a "real" home. In fact, they should feel they have two real homes with personal belongings at each.

- If a parent sends a list of clothing items and shoes to locate, the receiving parent should search for those items and respond within a reasonable time. If the response is "This item is not at my house," the requesting parent must accept that response and move on.

- Parents can enter a routine where the child always returns wearing the same outfit (and shoes) as they were wearing during the original exchange (with those items having been washed in the interim, if the length of the parenting time permits it). If Adam goes from Mom's house to Dad's wearing a Saints tee shirt, blue shorts, and blue tennis shoes and stays at Dad's house for five days, then on day 5 (exchange day), he should again be dressed in the Saints shirt, shorts, and shoes when he goes back to moms. This type of arrangement works for non-school day exchanges and may work on some school days as well. Even if Adam is of an age where he dresses himself, he can be encouraged to do this same-day dress for exchange days. Again, the exchange clothing should be laundered between exchange days.

- Parents can enter a routine where they periodically meet and exchange clothing, shoes, and outerwear that has piled up at the other parent's house. Some parents do this monthly or seasonally, and if there are pieces of clothing that are outgrown or neither parent wants, they are donated.

If the parents are unable to easily enter a routine about the child's clothing or find themselves sending numerous emails on the clothing issues, the following Plan language may be helpful:

Both parents will ensure that the child is dressed appropriately on exchange days in clean clothing of the appropriate size (including shoes). Each parent will monitor what clothing, personal property, and personal care items the child is transporting between homes and will endeavor to return items of clothing and personal property that the parent knows were purchased by the other parent, recognizing that it will not be possible to track each item of clothing. In general, if a parent purchases items of clothing for the child that the purchasing parent wants to remain in their home, the child should not be exchanged wearing those items. The parents agree that the child will transfer between homes along with the child's cell phone, iPad [list whatever items are agreed upon here].

Complaints about a child's clothing not fitting properly or being inappropriate are a different matter. In general, each parent is permitted to dress the child (or allow them to dress) as that parent deems appropriate, without input from the other parent. If a parent receives the child who is wearing ill-fitting shoes and clothing that is too small, the parent is not obligated to return them in the same ill-fitting clothing, but the ill-fitting clothing should be returned to the original parent with a note (an email sent close to the time of the exchange) saying that the clothing didn't fit so the child was not forced to wear those things again. It's helpful for a parent who buys the child new shoes to drop an email to the other parent to tell them what shoe size was purchased (even if those shoes aren't being transferred with the child).

D. Special Events and Sports Gear

A child may need to transport sports gear between homes and from school to practices and games. Sports gear can be bulky and heavy and duffel bags holding the gear can be far larger than backpacks. Schools can't always be expected to provide storage for sports gear during the school day, so parents may have to coordinate to have the gear transported from one parent's home to the other parent's home or directly to the practice or game location. Particularly, if a child rides the bus or is in a carpool, it's likely the child won't be able to maneuver a large bag of sports equipment through the school day, along with their own backpack and personal belongings. In those exceptional circumstances, this clause might be helpful:

> *During football season, the parents will need to cooperate to transfer the equipment, clothing, cleats, and other football paraphernalia between their homes so that the child is not expected to carry things to school. On each exchange day, the parent who is receiving the child to start parenting time will arrange to pick up the football-related equipment at the other parent's home (or another mutually agreed-upon location) not later than the end of the school day, and that parent with parenting time is responsible for transporting the equipment to the practice or game location.*

E. Forgotten Items

A Parenting Plan clause may need to define when the NCP can deliver items that a child forgot. The CP may feel that their time is unreasonably interrupted if the NCP "drops in," uninvited, to deliver a forgotten jacket or homework. It should be up to the CP to decide if a forgotten item is needed by the child. A sample clause for this situation, if one or both parents are violating boundaries and going to the other parent's home excessively, could be:

Exchange or delivery of children's personal items

Neither parent shall go to the other parent's home uninvited. If the child has left a personal item at the NCP'S home, the CP will be responsible for determining if the item is necessary and if so, for picking up that item at the NCP's home, office, or a mutually agreed-upon location. A child's personal items include their computer, iPad, phone, electronics or games, prescription medication, items of clothing, shoes, sports, or activity-related items. If the CP determines that an article of the child's personal property is at the NCP's home, the

CP will email the NCP and make arrangements to retrieve the items. The items must be exchanged personally between the parents and not left with a third party or at a third-party location to ensure the safety and delivery of the items. In no event will the NCP go to the CP's home without a specific written invitation. In no event will the parents have the child be the go-between to arrange for the delivery.

By leaving the decision about the item to the CP, that parent may decide to use the forgotten item as a learning experience for the child and have the child go without it for a while. This might encourage the child to remember everything the next time.

F. Child's Legal Paperwork

If court orders do not specify which parent is to retain important paperwork involving the child, such as birth certificates and social security cards, the parents should try to have the paperwork duplicated. Most states allow the issuance of a duplicate certified copy of a birth certificate so that each parent can have one in their possession. Social security cards may be able to be duplicated upon request. Both parents should have access to the child's social security number, which is necessary for tax filings. (See Child's Passport in Chapter 5.)

When considering how the parents can deal with or deliver the child's items between households, consider that, in most cases, these items belong to the child, not the parent. At some point, your child will grow into the ability to keep track of their own personal property and clothing items, but until then, the parents must figure out how to amicably resolve those issues and not put the child in the middle.

CHAPTER 12

Personal Care Decisions

The parents should consider and discuss that some personal care decisions for the child must be made by the parent with whom the child is living at a given time. We can call these types of decisions "personal care decisions," "day-to-day decisions," or "routine decisions." In all cases, we're talking about something that needs to be decided in the moment and which applies only for the immediate future (like one day) and does not include something that affects the child long-term. These decisions are usually not so major that they require both parents to agree.

A. What is a Routine Decision?

The most common examples of day-to-day or routine decisions include: whether a child will be given an over-the-counter medication like cough medicine or Tylenol; whether the child is sick enough to stay home from school; what time the child will go to bed, and whether they need a bath that night; or what type of routine discipline should be used for minor infractions in that home. Those types of decisions are usually made by the parent with whom the child is living, and while notice of these things should often be given to the other parent, the other parent doesn't need to agree with them.

In contrast, having a child vaccinated is a more permanent decision and involves more than just one parent's parenting time, so that becomes a decision which should be discussed between parents and agreed upon. If there is no agreement, some method of dispute resolution will be needed. (See Dispute Resolution in Chapter 17.)

Some state laws recognize that there are day-to-day, routine decisions to be made by just one parent. Arizona's law, for example, says,

> [ARS 25-401(5)] "'Parenting time' means the schedule of time during which each parent has access to a child at specified times. Each parent during their scheduled parenting time is responsible for providing the child with food, clothing and shelter and may make routine decisions concerning the child's care."

The NCP should not try to influence how the CP will handle those specific situations that apply only to the CP's home. While the NCP should receive notice of some of these things (such as a missed day of school or the use of over-the-counter medication), that doesn't mean the NCP participates in the decision. And, if a child's discipline in one home includes loss of the use of a phone, the child still must be given use of a phone to speak with the other parent when scheduled. Discipline cannot include cutting off access to the other parent through grounding or confiscating a phone.

B. Temporary versus Permanent Decisions

Personal care decisions that affect the child over a longer time frame can be a source of conflict. Decisions about a child's personal appearance which are relatively permanent, i.e. piercings (putting holes in the skin) or tattoos (adding indelible ink), must always be made jointly. Less permanent changes, including haircuts and non-permanent hair color, are less disruptive and are likely day-to-day decisions to be made by one parent or the other.

Co-parents may disagree about what constitutes a temporary versus permanent change to a child's appearance. Putting on a temporary henna tattoo is a routine decision, but getting a permanent tattoo is not. Permanently changing a child's hair color is not a routine one-parent decision, but putting in a temporary color that washes out in one shampoo is. Haircuts involve a gray area. Having a child get a trim of an inch or so is probably a routine, day-to-day decision, but changing a child's hairstyle drastically, going to a crew cut, cutting off several inches of hair, or getting a mohawk would not be a routine decision one parent can make on their own. In high-conflict cases, court orders may specify when a child's hair may be cut and which parent takes them to the barber or salon.

A parent who permits a relatively permanent change to a child's appearance without the other parent's permission will often be subject to court sanctions, which could include the loss of some decision-making rights. Drastically changing a child's hair or appearance just before a special event occurs with the other parent is particularly bad form. Family courts are very familiar with the situation where one parent's remarriage is coming up, and the other parent suddenly decides to give the child a drastic change in hairstyle, such as cutting off long hair, or getting a mullet. Those types of radical changes to a child's appearance are considered detrimental to the child and against their best interests and, again, can result in sanctions against the offending parent.

C. Are Religious Decisions Routine?

Religious decisions can be both routine as well as serious. Some decisions must be made jointly by the parents. While most courts will not interfere with a parent's right to engage in the religion they want with the child during their own parenting time, including having the child attend a religious service, courts can and will place restrictions on more serious religious activities. Major decisions such as ceremonies or inductions into a religion are likely so serious that they require joint discussion and decision-making by both parents. Neither parent should initiate a child's bar or bat mitzvah, baptism, confirmation, or otherwise entered into a given status in a religion without at least notifying and discussing the issue with the other parent well in advance. If the parents are in serious opposition regarding religions (or lack of same), it may be that each parent is restricted to having the child active in their religion only on a day-to–day basis, during their own parenting time.

There is often a fine line between what is a day-to-day (routine) decision versus a decision that must be discussed and agreed upon with the other parent. When in doubt, ask your attorney or do more research, or simply talk to the other parent. If it appears a decision involves only your own parenting time and does not result in a permanent change of appearance or status for the child, that could be a day-to-day decision you can make on your own.

CHAPTER 13

Child's Social Media and Device Use

Addressing social media and device use for children is crucial to ensure a cohesive and consistent approach to the child's digital well-being. Effective provisions may include establishing guidelines for age-appropriate screen time, emphasizing responsible online behavior, and promoting open communication between co-parents regarding the child's digital activities. Everything to do with social media and online activity changes constantly, and new challenges about these things will arise – often.

Your Parenting Plan might specify rules for the use of social media platforms, taking into account the child's age and maturity level. The Plan might outline provisions for monitoring online content and interactions, while also encouraging the development of healthy offline activities. Consistency in rules and expectations between both households is best to provide stability for the child. The Plan may include provisions for periodic reviews and adjustments as the child gets older and their digital needs evolve.

Ultimately, a well-crafted Parenting Plan on social media and device use aims to foster a safe and supportive online environment while promoting shared responsibility and communication between divorced co-parents.

A. Online Safety

When the separating parents have a very young child (infant, preschool, early elementary years), it may not occur to them to discuss (at the time of their original Plan) exactly when their child will be ready for social media, an iPad, a cell phone, etc. Most Parenting Plans for very young children can only cover how the parents will deal with those issues when the time comes.

When parents are at the point when they need to discuss a child's use of devices and social media, the areas for discussion should include:

- What parental controls or apps each parent is using in their home? Does either parent use a monitoring app or device? Examples of these apps as of this writing include Bark, Quotsdio, FamiSafe, Norton Family, Smart Family, Life 360 and Family Where.

- What social media accounts have each parent allowed the child to sign up for, or which ones does the child already have? What are each social media site's age requirements for opening an account? The specific online provider's requirements should be followed. At this writing, Facebook, Instagram, TikTok, and Snapchat all state that a person must be 13 years old to have an account, and X's age requirement is 15. If one parent assists a child younger than those requirements in opening an account, the other parent may object and request court intervention.

- The names of video games the child uses regularly and the login information (if any) to those games. Parents should be aware of what chat functions are available in the video game and who the child is chatting with while playing. Also, parents may want to consider whether a game is age appropriate, and that is indicated on the game's packaging or on the app store where the game was obtained.

- How many minutes or hours per day the child is allowed to be online, gaming, or using a device.

- Where the devices remain at night. Is the child allowed to take a phone, game, or device to bed, or do the devices remain in the main living area? Are the parents aware if a child is staying awake late at night playing video games?

The discussion of appropriate parental controls for online use could fill a book on its own, and there are several books to help parents with online safety concerns.[45]

B. Access to the Child's Online Accounts

Your Parenting Plan should include provisions so both parents can monitor the child's online access and use. The rules are fairly straightforward when it comes to a child's login information: if a parent opens a social media, gaming, or any type of online account for a child, that login information should be provided to the other parent simultaneously with opening the account. Each parent should have login information for all the child's accounts, and that information should be stored in a place available to both parents. Passwords, usernames, and passcodes to a child's devices and apps should not be changed by one parent unless the new ones are immediately provided to the other parent.

C. Privacy

A child's use of technology can pose privacy concerns for divorced or separated parents. Each parent needs to know the following:

- what devices are in the other parent's home and in your child's possession or control.

- how to secure those devices or at least know what's going on with them.

Problems can arise when one parent has the child's login information connected with that parent's overall account. For example, when setting up an Apple account, a child's account name may be associated with the parent's (or parent's household) Apple account, and access to the child's Apple account could open information from the parent's account as well. If you have Apple or Android products in your home, you should be familiar with how a shared Apple or Google account could inadvertently reveal information. Every family lawyer has a story about how a parent has passed on an old device (IOS or Android) to a child and found out, too late, that all the parent's emails, texts, photos, and other information were also passed on to the child (and taken to the other parent's house). Co-parents should consider not attaching a child's account to their own account. Instead, create an entirely separate account that both parents may access.

How is each parent locking their personal devices to make sure a child doesn't access parent devices, search histories, parental apps like Our Family Wizard or Talking Parents, and other accounts? Parents should have separate login information that isn't known to the child to keep parent information private.

Parents should consider at what point parental monitoring turns into stalking or unlawful tracking of the other parent. Are GPS devices being used to protect the children or to monitor the whereabouts of the other parent? To address this concern, parents should pledge that neither will use a child or a child's possession to send a GPS tracking device to the other parent's home without notice. This applies to Gizmo, Gabb, and Apple watches and similar devices. If tracking or "Find my phone" is enabled on a device, both parents should know of this. Some of the tracking mechanisms that could be used in a child's belongings could result in criminal stalking charges.

As discussed in Chapter 11, Plan language to cover this situation could be:

Neither parent will send the child to the other parent's home with any type of tracking or GPS-related device unless the other parent is specifically informed. Examples of these items include a child's cell phone, a Gizmo or Apple watch, an Air-Tag, any device with a "Find Me" app enabled, or any type of GPS tracker (placed on either the child's person or in a personal property item).

While the parents are discussing these issues, they should also consider how each parent has the other's information entered in Contacts in their cell phones. If Mother's information is entered as "Psycho bitch" or Father's entered as "Worthless Scum," or if nasty emojis are used, your children are seeing these names and images. The court will eventually see them, too, and there will be consequences for the offending parent. More importantly, the child's self-esteem will be harmed by seeing their Mother's name shown as "Golddigger" on Dad's phone.

The parents can discuss and agree to a Technology Agreement, in addition to their Parenting Plan. By making this a separate document, the document can be personalized and updated based on what social media and devices are being used by the child at a given time. (See Sample Technology Agreement in Appendix 4.)

Dealing with your child's social media and online activity is one of the more challenging areas for parents, and one challenge is that this environment is constantly changing. Parents need to review and update their knowledge of the child's online activity almost constantly and need to keep each other informed of what activity is allowed in each home.

CHAPTER 14

Driver's License and Driver Education

When a child reaches age 15 ½ - 16, assuming the child shows interest in getting a driver's license, the parents must cooperate in making decisions. Initially, the notion that a driver's license is a privilege and not a right must be acknowledged by the parents and communicated to the child. While a child has a right to certain things (safe homes, education, health care), a child does not have a right to have a driver's license without showing they are ready.

As with social media use, parents entering a Parenting Plan for a very young child may not be close to considering the parameters for a drivers' license which is years off. The questions and suggested language below may be something the parents need to address as a modification and addendum to their original Plan, when the time comes.

Some of the things you must consider with your co-parent regarding a child's driver's license are:

- In getting a license, it is usually the case that each parent has the opportunity to drive with the child individually to assess their driving skills and maturity behind the wheel. Do both parents spend enough time with the child to be able to assess driving skills?

- Can the parents agree on using a driver education school, and if so, who pays for it?

- Operating a vehicle safely requires a high degree of stability in one's life. Are most things in the child's life stable, including the child's relationship with both parents, school performance, other relationships, and other activities?

- Does the child have a need for a license and driving, including long distances between the parents' homes or the need for transportation to activities or employment?

- Do the parents agree on the basics of driving rules for the child?

- Can they drive at night, or are there restricted hours?

- Can they drive with teenagers, and if so, how many in the car?

- Can they drive their younger siblings, and under what circumstances?

- Are there any restrictions on where they can drive? Can they drive on freeways and out of town, and under what circumstances?

- Will any type of monitoring device (for speed, etc.) be installed on the vehicles they're driving? If so, what are the consequences for violating the speed or other safety measures?

- What vehicles are they permitted to drive? If the child is to be given a designated vehicle, will they drive it back and forth between the two households, and will they become responsible for all of their own (and possibly their siblings') exchanges?

- Who will pay car insurance, and which vehicles have specific coverage for the child?

- What happens if they have a fender bender and cause damage to one of your cars or someone else's vehicle or property?
- What happens if they get a speeding ticket or other violation? Who pays? Is the ability to drive restricted as a result?

In the event the parents can't agree on all aspects of the child getting a license and driving, a situation may arise where the child is allowed to drive while at one parent's home but not at the other's. It is doubtful that either parent can be forced by court orders (or by the other parent) to allow a child to drive while the child lives in their home, over that parent's objection.

An example of a driver's license clause for your Plan could be:

The parents agree the child should, with proper training, be permitted to apply for and obtain a driver's license. At a minimum the child shall meet the classroom and in-vehicle instruction requirements set forth by the [State's] Department of Transportation. Upon completion, both parents shall sign and notarize the necessary application for the child's driver's license. Neither parent will unreasonably withhold their signature and consent.

CHAPTER 15

Special Circumstances

Arguably, almost everything to do with raising a child with a co-parent is "special," but there are some distinct situations that call for additional language and extra attention. A few of these situations include the relocation of a parent (with or without the child), the need for a long-distance Parenting Plan with its related problems (such as last-minute changes to the schedule, missing school, and the child's travel to see that parent), a child's reluctance to go for parenting time, a parent's substance abuse, and when a parent's parenting time must be supervised.

A. Relocation

Relocation means one (or both) parents desire to relocate from the area where they have been residing with the child and want to take the child with them. Relocation can mean the child will change from local (same city) exchanges to long-distance exchanges that could require several hours of driving or flights. Relocation with a child usually means the child's school will need to be changed, and one parent will be forced to spend substantially less time with the child on school days and during the school year.

In most jurisdictions, relocation requires substantial proof from the parent who wants to relocate that the relocation/move will benefit the child. Parents sometimes ask to relocate based on personal preferences or may make the request based on a job transfer that is either involuntary or for a job change that provides advancement for the parent (higher wages, better job conditions, more opportunity for advancement, etc.) that to decline the transfer would be difficult. Some relocations are based on the parent remarrying, and the new partner is employed or based in another state. Some vocations are simply more available and more lucrative in other locations.

The parents may reach agreements when one parent needs to relocate by renegotiating their Parenting Plan and setting up a different parenting schedule. If the parents can't agree on this, the decision about a new Plan, or whether the child may relocate with the moving parent, will need to be left up to the court. Even when the parents have an agreement, existing court orders need to be changed to reflect the new schedule.

Relocation decisions are very difficult for the court and very difficult to mediate, as compromises on locations are hard to come by. Usually, the best compromise offer that the relocating parent can make is to offer substantial parenting time to the parent left behind during non-school periods. That type of long-distance Parenting Plan would leave the non-replaced parent with most of the school breaks (spring, fall, and at least half of winter break) and most of the summer break. The relocating parent then must accept that they will be left with little non-school time with the child and little time to vacation with the child.

The cost of travel must be considered in any relocation discussion, as the child may be flying between homes frequently. For young children, the cost must consider the cost of a parent/other adult traveling with the child on the plane, or the cost of Unaccompanied Minors. (See Chapter 5.)

One common resolution for travel costs is that the child's travel expenses are divided in proportion to each parent's income (similar to a child support calculation). Or the parent who is relocating with the child may agree to pay the child's travel expenses as a condition of being allowed to relocate.

B. LONG DISTANCE PARENTING TIME

If you and your co-parent live far apart, you'll need to consider the issue of long-distance parenting time.

Sample Long-Distance Plans

When one parent (the long-distance parent) lives a significant distance from the child's home area, where the child lives with the other parent and attends school, a typical long-distance Plan would provide that the child will be with the long-distance parent for spring break, or fall break, or both; and at least half of winter break from school, and for the majority of the summer break. An example of summer break time division might be where a child has a ten-week school break for summer, six or seven of those weeks will be spent at the long-distance parent's location, leaving two to three weeks for the child to live and vacation with the other parent, including a week or two to get ready for the start of the next school year. It's usually optimal that the child be back in their home area (where they go to school) at least one week prior to the first day of school in the fall semester. A child's activities or school orientation days may require that a child be back in their home area even earlier than that.

When determining the summer break parenting time, the child's age is important. If the child is very young, the parents may want to consider dividing the long-distance parent's time into two summer blocks, with a block of one to two weeks with the other parent in the middle, so that the child is not away from either parent for an extended period.

In addition to the break periods, the long-distance parent may be able to have the child in their area for one long weekend per month, and the long-distance parent may be assigned parenting time for most of the 3-day weekends shown on the school calendar. The long-distance parent is usually also given some specific parenting time (say, a full weekend) anytime they can visit the child's home area during the school year, with advance notice to the other parent. The Plan may state that the long-distance parent can have at least one weekend per month by coming to the child's home area, and that weekend may be specified ("the second weekend of each month, with weekend defined as beginning on the 2nd Friday of each month"), or the long-distance parent may be required to give reasonable advance notice of when they can be in the child's home area. Reasonable advance notice can differ depending on the child's age and whether the child is regularly involved in activities, but it should be at least 14 days advance notice. When the long-distance parent is visiting in the child's home area, it is usually expected that the long-distance parent will stay at an Airbnb, appropriate friend or family member's house, or hotel and take the child to any regularly scheduled activities like extracurriculars, lessons, school activities, or planned parties.

The school calendar is more important than ever when it comes to a long-distance parenting arrangement. How the school calendar handles days off for fall break and Thanksgiving may determine what parenting time the long-distance parent has during October and November. Some school districts take off the entire week of Thanksgiving for that holiday, combining that holiday with fall break. Other districts have a more traditional fall break of 3-5 days in either October or November. Some districts have no school on the Wednesday prior to Thanksgiving, while other districts will have school in session until noon or 3 pm that Wednesday. Determining how the child's school district handles those holiday and break periods will help determine what break time should be awarded to the long-distance parent.

The older a child gets, the more likely they are to resist some of the extended time periods away from their home area. Teenagers, in general, start to spend less and less time with either parent, no matter which home they're in, and the child will want the parenting time schedule to focus on their needs and interests, including being with friends, having a job, and attending extracurriculars and sports. When a child shows resistance or refusal to travel to the long-distance parent's home, the long-distance parent may take the resistance personally when this attitude has little to do with the parent and everything to do with the child's need for autonomy. At this point, having both the child and long-distance parent engaged in counseling (even by virtual/remote means) may help the family understand the child's need for independence from a strict parenting time schedule. When a child becomes mature enough to specifically state their needs and ask the parents not to force them to strictly comply with a written Plan, that child's needs should be considered. (See Should the Child Be Interviewed? in Chapter 5.)

Substantial Parenting Time Plan for the Long Distance Parent with a Typical School Schedule

January
Friday to Monday over MLK Weekend

February
Friday to Monday over President's Day Weekend

March
Saturday to Sunday of Spring Break

April
Friday to Sunday on a parent-selected weekend

May
Friday to Monday over Memorial Day Weekend

June
June 9th to July 21st (6 weeks)

July
June 9th to July 21st (6 weeks)

August
Friday to Sunday on a parent-selected weekend

September
Friday to Monday over Labor Day Weekend

October
Saturday to Sunday of Fall Break

November
Odd-numbered years from Wednesday to Sunday over Thanksgiving

December
First half of winter break in even-numbered years, and second half in odd-numbered years

Travel

To make a long-distance parenting schedule work, the parents will need to discuss whether the child can fly back and forth between homes without an adult. Airlines call this flying status as an Unaccompanied Minor (UM). Until the child is ready for UM flying, a parent or adult will need to fly with them for all exchanges. Sometimes, the parent who is retrieving the child will make the trip with the child, which results in each parent making one round trip for each long-distance period. How the parents' airfare is paid needs to be decided by the parents or by the court, and that will depend on the parents' respective financial circumstances and whether one parent or the other caused the long-distance travel to be necessary.

Parents may disagree on whether a child is ready to fly as a UM. If the child has a counselor, that counselor may be used to help determine a child's readiness. A child's readiness for UM flying will depend on the child's overall maturity, how each parent approaches the issue with the child, the child's flying experience with each parent and the family, and the length of the flight. When a child needs to change planes or make connections, the issue of UM flying becomes more complicated and may require more preparation than a non-stop flight. Some airlines may simply not permit connecting flights for UMs, as the airline is required to provide extra personnel to accompany a UM between flights.

Each airline has its own policies about how two children (either both under the age of 14 or one over and one under 14) can fly together and what additional fees will be charged for multiple children flying together (but without an adult).

Last-Minute Trips by the Long-Distance Parent

If a long-distance parent can arrange to be in the child's home area at the last minute (not a regularly scheduled time as discussed above), it's a good idea to try to find time for additional parenting time for the long-distance parent. Even last-minute notice of the ability to be in the child's home area can usually be accommodated so long as the long-distance parent makes sure the child still attends school and regularly scheduled activities and appointments.

Consider both sides:

Annette: The "home parent" believes last-minute trips by the out-of-town parent are too intrusive and chaotic, especially for younger children. The children have a right to their set schedules without being interrupted at the last minute. The child could be upset to know he will miss baseball practice if Dad comes to town.

Nicole: The long-distance parent should see their child whenever they are in the area! Isn't access to a parent more important than activities?

There's no easy answer to this question. Some children need great stability with parenting time and need to know with some specificity when they'll be seeing a parent. Similarly, that child may need to know that they're going to be attending baseball practice without any interruptions. Other children will do just fine with unexpected and last-minute parenting time. As with so many things, there is no right answer, and it all depends on the child. But it is reasonable for a long-distance parent who is making a last-minute trip to take the child to all scheduled activities, or the child may resent the visit.

Missing School or Special Events

When a long-distance Parenting Plan is prepared, the parents need to discuss whether the child will miss school or activities (like sports) in order to travel to the long-distance parent. The parents may agree that, with the school's consent, the child may miss one Friday per month or a set number of Fridays per semester in order to make travel to the long-distance parent's home easier on the child. Neither parent should take the child out of school for long-distance travel (or otherwise) without the permission of the other parent and advance permission from the school and the teachers involved. Schools and teachers tend to be accommodating for infrequent absences (or early releases) if arrangements are made to make up any substantive work.

C. Parent-Child Contact Problems (PCCP)

The issue of PCCP is discussed in more detail in Chapter 2. There are no simple definitions or simple resolutions to a case involving PCCP characteristics, and the myriad of potential causes of parental rejection show that a child's refusal to engage in a relationship with a parent is a family systems issue, with usually more than one cause.

In general, developing and following a good, detailed Parenting Plan is a first step to avoid these contact problems. If both parents follow the Plan, keep up with their respective responsibilities under the Plan, and communicate effectively with each other, many of the reasons for a child's resistance can be avoided.

A number of court and therapeutic systems have been put in place to try to deal with PCCP, including the use of counselors, therapists, joint therapists (sometimes called "therapeutic interventionists" or "interventionists"), and programs to try to improve the relationship between a parent and child. Most of these programs utilize long-recognized therapeutic processes (which are research-based), including desensitization and exposure therapy, cognitive behavioral therapy, psychoeducation, and emotional regulation work. These therapies in general can't be effective until there is a determination that the issues of domestic violence and child abuse have been ruled out.

If the parents can't agree on therapy (usually including all family members), the parent who wants to have the contact problems addressed and the parenting time orders enforced will have to ask the court for relief.

D. Domestic Violence

Where domestic violence (DV, also sometimes called intimate partner violence or IPV) exists in a relationship, the first rules of parenting time and a Parenting Plan are the safety of the child and both parents.

DV/IPV comes in many forms and many degrees of intensity. DV/IPV may be considered "significant," or be a history of domestic violence, or be situational or short-term domestic violence, such as a single and sudden outburst in the heat of an argument. This is not to minimize even a single outburst – all DV/IPV is wrong and serious when it comes to the victim and the child.

Although it may seem unfair, if domestic violence has only occurred between the parents and has not posed a direct physical danger to the child, the court may order parenting time between the perpetrator and the child so long as the parents do not have unsupervised contact with each other.[46] In this way, the victim of DV/IPV will not be exposed to the perpetrator, and the child will not be exposed to conflict or violence between the parents.

To allow parenting time to happen, the exchanges of the child will occur only through school or childcare, so the parents are not in the same location at the same time. When school is not in session or childcare is closed, the parents may need to use third parties to make the exchanges, or in extreme cases, hire an exchange supervisor who physically takes the child from one location to the other.

Parents sometimes can agree to curbside exchanges, particularly if the child is old enough to walk by themselves from one parent to the other, leaving substantial distance between the parents during exchanges. The parents should not communicate or have any type of interaction during these exchanges. (See Public Place Exchanges and Curbside Exchanges in Chapter 5.)

When DV/IPV has been an issue, the parents' communication with each other should be limited by the Plan or court order, such that either their emails are reviewed by a third party or follow strict guidelines. Some types of restraining orders mandate that the parents may have email communication "only about the child," and both parents should assume that their communications will be reviewed by a court or law enforcement to assess violations. In cases where a perpetrator continues to send inappropriate, threatening, harassing emails or emails that violate court restraining orders, a service known as Propercomm (www.propercomm. com) acts as an intermediary to receive emails from one parent, review and edit them as necessary, and forward them to the other parent. Inappropriate emails that need to be edited incur charges, so this service also acts as a coaching device to teach parents to limit their email contact to appropriate contact that is solely about the child.

If the DV/IPV is deemed by the court to be of enough significance to warrant direct protection of the child, supervision of parenting time may be ordered. (See Supervised Parenting Time in Chapter 15.)

Courts have various tools to deal with DV/IPV cases involving children. Perpetrators may be ordered to take classes including anger management and behavior modification and to get education to show the effects of DV/IPV on children. Screening for domestic violence is the first step, followed by assessment of the extent of the family exposure to violence, then focusing on the effects of the violence and responding to the family's needs for intervention. [47] Screening and assessment of DV/IPV will help the victim and the courts determine what parenting time, if any, is appropriate in the circumstances and what safety measures are necessary to protect the victim and the child.

E. Substance Abuse by a Parent

A parent's substance use significantly impacts the well-being and safety of a child, particularly when the parents are separated. To safeguard the child, specific provisions and rigorous testing requirements are necessary to monitor abstinence, at least during parenting time. A brief overview of some types of testing and considerations for parents seeking to address substance abuse testing in their Parenting Plans is included here. Both parents involved in a case where substance abuse has been an issue should familiarize themselves with testing procedures and what happens when a parent tests positive (or misses a required test) for a substance that's being monitored or is prohibited under their Plan.

Alcohol testing (also called "EtG" testing, for Ethyl Glucuronide) has improved over the years to the point that companies like Soberlink and BACtrack provide Bluetooth devices and software that allow for remote breath alcohol content monitoring with tests transmitted in real time through a cell phone and which include photos/videos of the testing person to ensure no tampering has occurred. Testing may occur on a set schedule, only when the parents have the children, or randomly at any time. These devices are effective in monitoring alcohol use, but they also allow for a parent's freedom of movement and are used regularly in family law proceedings. The parents must, however, consider the expense. Both BACtrack and Soberlink require the purchase of a device and payment of a separate monitoring plan for the device.

A Parenting Plan will need to include terms addressing:

- The payment of the costs associated with BACtrack or Soberlink.

- The correct use of the device and schedule for use of the device.

- How and when test results are received by the other parent and/or the court.

The following is an example of testing language requiring BACtrack or Soberlink testing immediately before a parent exercises parenting time and when a parent is exercising parenting time. However, we suggest you review the draft language available on either company's website that address specific features related to the specific device and plan:

Alcohol monitoring will be obtained through [name of company] using their testing device. Parent B shall pay all the costs associated with the device and testing. Two hours before the start of Parent B's parenting time, Parent B shall submit a test upon waking between 8:00 am and 9:00 pm, during the middle of the day between 12:00 pm and 1:00 pm, and before bed between 9:00 pm and 10:00 pm. Any test submitted outside of the above testing windows is considered missed. Parent A shall be listed as a contact and receive emailed test results in real time. Parent B shall review all instructions before activating their device. Parent B will follow all testing protocols.

Drug testing has not reached the same level of ease as alcohol testing. There have been advancements in drug testing, but most tests still require the testing party to appear in person at a testing facility. Monitored urinalysis tests at drug testing centers (usually associated with the court system and done by court order) remain the most widely used and effective method for drug testing. In addition to urinalysis, other types of testing include hair, blood, oral fluid, nail, and even sweat testing. Drug testing through these methods is effective when a parent is tested during a drug detection window (a certain amount of time). Detection windows vary depending on the type of drug and the amount and frequency of the alleged drug use. Hair and nail testing generally allows detection of substances for longer periods of time than urinalysis but will not detect use for a period right before a test.

Drug testing issues arise when a parent's sample is diluted, tampered with, or shows false positive or false negative. Follow-up testing, usually some form of gas chromatography testing, can determine if a result was valid. To prevent tampering in the process of testing, personal observation of the test is recommended.

Parents should consider the type of testing, who provides it, and the procedures for testing. In addition, a well-written order or Parenting Plan will address when a positive, diluted, or missed test occurs, such as suspended or missed parenting time. Other questions that should be answered in the order or Plan include: what happens if a false positive occurs; is makeup parenting time an option? The answers to these issues will vary between cases, but they are areas that need to be discussed before the Plan is finalized.

A testing parent will need to document compliance with drug testing and other treatment. Generally, if a child's best interests are at issue, a parent's medical records concerning rehabilitation or treatment will be discoverable in the court proceedings.

SMART Recover (Self-Management and Recovery Training), Alcoholics Anonymous (AA), or Al-Anon (and related Narcotics Anonymous (NA) or Nar-Anon meetings) are distinct organizations that provide support and resources for individuals and their loved ones dealing with alcohol-related issues, as well as other addictive behaviors including drugs and gambling. SMART provides a secular program with meetings and support. AA provides support for the substance-abusing parent, and Al-Anon provides support for family and friends of individuals with alcohol challenges. AA meetings, in general, will not provide evidence of attendance at meetings (as meetings are anonymous), and for that reason a court order requiring proof of AA meeting attendance is likely not a helpful order. However, SMART may be willing to provide some sort of evidence of a parent's attendance.

Drug or alcohol testing provisions require detail and should include, at a minimum, the following:

- Agency or drug testing location.

- Scope of the test, including which drugs will be tested or screened.

- Required cooperation by the testing parent, including providing samples and following directions, presenting ID, and signing all releases for the results to be released as agreed by the parties.

- Cost of the test and who will pay.

- How and to whom the results will be reported, and whether the court will be alerted.

- Frequency of testing includes whether it will occur only when they are with the child or on a random basis.

- What will occur when there is a positive, diluted, or missed test, and whether it will affect parenting time.

- What will occur if there is a false positive.

- Whether a parent is required to attend other services or groups to address their addiction and how that attendance will be monitored or proven.

F. Supervised Parenting Time

Sometimes a parent's time with the child must be supervised for the child's safety. A parent with substance abuse or mental illness problems or a parent who has committed child abuse or DV/IPV will be monitored until the child's safety is ensured. A parent who has wrongfully taken the child may be monitored to ensure the child is returned from parenting time. At times, a child's discomfort or lack of history with a parent or a child's allegations of abuse by a parent may call for supervised parenting time for the protection of the parent as well as the child.

Supervision can be provided by professional supervisors or agencies or, in some cases, by a family member or friend who is able and willing to monitor the child's safety. Where serious allegations about a parent's violence or criminal activity exist, or where a child has been abducted by the parent previously, supervision should be done only at a specific agency location that provides safety measures such as metal detectors and security personnel. The parent and child do not leave the secured agency building during the visit.

Some supervised visits may be made in the community, including at parks, public places, shopping malls, and movie theaters, with the supervisor present at all times. The supervisor may provide transportation to the visitation site so that the parents are never in the same vicinity. The supervisor will generally meet the child in advance of the first supervised visit to establish rapport.

Whether the supervisor is a professional or a non-professional family member or friend, the following general provisions are followed during supervised parenting time:

- The child is never alone with the supervised parent.

- The supervisor accompanies the child for all restroom visits.

- The supervisor can terminate the visit early if anything inappropriate occurs.

- The supervisor is usually available as a witness and may provide a written report about the visits.

- The supervisor does not allow any secret communications between the supervised parent and the child – no whispering, passing notes, unusual body language, or foreign language.

- The supervisor does not allow the supervised parent to talk to the child about the court case or about the other parent or other parent's home.

- The supervisor can cancel or terminate the visit if the supervisor believes the parent to be under the influence of alcohol or drugs or behaves badly, shows anger, makes threats, or refuses to follow rules for the monitored visit.

- The supervisor needs to be a neutral person who does not have strong alliances with either parent and whose primary concern is the safety and well-being of the child.

- The supervisor should be willing to execute a Safety Agreement or other court-approved document outlining the rules of supervision and their responsibilities and willingness to comply with those responsibilities.

If a professional supervisor or agency is used, the costs of supervision must be allocated; either the supervised parent will be responsible for those costs, or the parties will share in those costs in some proportion. If the supervised parenting time takes place in public places, the costs of supervision will include any costs attributable to the supervisor, such as movie tickets or admission to an activity. Most professional supervisors charge for travel time as well as time following the visits to write a report about the visit for the use of the parents and court.

This chapter addresses a variety of special circumstances that require more thought and detail in a Parenting Plan. Parents should keep in mind that their situation is unique, and they should be willing to discuss and agree on modifications to provisions suggested here to fit their own situation. PCs or skilled mediators can be of great help in working through the most difficult situations.

CHAPTER 16

Reimbursement of Expenses

While this book is not intended to deal with financial issues between the parents, the issue of reimbursements owed from one parent to the other for child-related expenses is often a problem, and has such an effect on co-parenting, that it must be mentioned. If you are drawing up your own Parenting Plan, be sure to address reimbursement.

By reimbursements, we mean the possibility that one parent owes money to the other for a child-related expense such as a medical bill, prescription, extracurricular expense, dues, tutoring, sports equipment, travel, school supplies, yearbook, a cell phone and phone plan, and many other expenses that a child incurs in daily life. Reimbursements can also be an issue for more esoteric expenses like college applications and testing (SATs, etc.) that happen during high school, college tuition payments for dual-enrollment classes taken during high school, a computer or iPad, GED expenses, cord blood storage, car insurance, or the cost of a car itself.

The amount of each parent's responsibility for reimbursement depends on your agreement and your jurisdiction's laws. The parents might be equally (50-50) responsible for expenses, or they might be responsible in proportion to their income. If Father makes $40,000 per year and Mother makes $80,000, then Father's proportionate amount might be 33% and Mother's proportionate amount 67%, based on earnings.

Just because an item is listed above doesn't mean reimbursement is owed from one parent to the other. Some of the listed items (a car, car insurance, or a cell phone) may be considered optional, and if one parent chooses to provide that to a child, the other parent may not be required to contribute to that expense. If a computer or certain books are required by the school, that increases the chances that the parents should share in that expense in some proportion, but if not specifically required by a school, those items are more likely considered optional, no matter how beneficial those things are for the child. Each jurisdiction has different laws about what extras might be considered optional and what expenses must be paid by the parents. Some jurisdictions may consider a cell phone or car insurance to be something the child must have and, therefore, will allocate the expense. You will need to check the laws in your jurisdiction to find out what you might be responsible for.

In general, if medical expenses are incurred for a child and those expenses are reasonably and medically necessary, court orders probably state that the parents are jointly responsible for those expenses, possibly in percentages proportionate to each parent's income. Some "medical" expenses won't be reasonably necessary. For example, taking the child to a chiropractor for an adjustment may not be considered a reasonably necessary medical expense.

Don't assume that the other parent owes you for every expense related to the child. Before making demands on the other parent for reimbursement, get legal advice about whether a reimbursement might be owed. If your Parenting Plan says that the parents will share the cost of a cell phone for the child, then reimbursement is probably owed, but if that specific language doesn't appear in your court orders, a cell phone is probably considered to be optional. If Parent A wants the child to have a cell phone, then Parent A will be expected to pay for all of it.

Similarly, payments for things like school lunches or school supplies may not be considered separate reimbursements if those items are presumed to be part of a child support payment. A child's day-to-day clothing needs, personal items, sundries, over-the-counter medications, and general transportation for the child during parenting time are probably considered to be things paid for by the CP or part of a child support award.

When a parent is satisfied that an expense should be partially reimbursed by the other parent, the expense should be submitted with a request for a specific amount. A receipt showing the total expense incurred, with a description of the expense and the date incurred should be provided, along with proof that the amount was paid, and a request for a specific amount of money.

Examples:

"Attached is the invoice for Charlie's visit to Dr. Smith on 10-1-2022. The total amount was $110.00, and the receipt shows that I paid this in full. Per our court orders, your portion is 50%, so please reimburse me for $55.00 for this expense."

"Attached is the receipt dated 9-5-2022 showing that I paid $50.00 for Charlie's Cub Scout dues for the year 2022-23. We agreed on this expense and activity in our emails dated April 23 and 25, 2022, and agreed that we would equally share this expense. Please reimburse me for your half, $25.00."

Court procedures may require that you submit expenses within a certain period, such as within six months of when the expense was incurred. You should seek legal advice to find out:

- If time periods apply to your case.
- To see if a particular expense is subject to reimbursement or if it's optional or covered by child support.

- To find out if there are specific requirements about what you need to submit to be reimbursed.

- What to do if reimbursements are not paid.

If you receive a request for reimbursement from the other parent and you do not believe it to be something you should reimburse, or you think the request doesn't have enough information, you should respond to the other parent with a specific objection to the item:

Examples:

"I received your request for reimbursement for lunch money paid for September and October. There are no court orders stating that I should reimburse you for lunch expenses, and each of us is required to supply Charlie with food during our own parenting time. I will not be reimbursing this amount."

"I received your request for reimbursement for medicine for Charlie. There is nothing to show what was purchased as you sent only a Walgreens receipt showing payment of $31.00 for something. If you submit an itemized receipt showing that you paid for a prescription for Charlie, what the prescribed medicine was, and the date and amount, I will reimburse you my portion."

Finally, a very comprehensive Plan clause for reimbursements could be something like this. Note that this clause has two time periods for reimbursement requests each year. The parents can also agree to request reimbursements once per quarter or once per month. The period for requesting should take into account how much money is usually spent on these items so that neither parent has to wait a long time for reimbursement of significant amounts.

Reimbursement of child expenses. The parents agree to share expenses for the children in these categories: uninsured medical, dental, optical, orthodontia, and psychological/therapy expenses for the child; and agreed-upon extracurricular expenses, including sports fees, uniforms, equipment, travel, lessons, and similar items.

The extracurricular expenses will be shared for those activities in which the parents agree in writing. A parent who undertakes an extracurricular or similar expense without a specific written agreement for sharing the expense takes the risk that they may be entirely responsible for that expense.

The child's medical and related expenses shall be expenses that are reasonably and medically necessary for the child.

The expenses that are subject to sharing and reimbursement are shared with Mother responsible for ___% and Father responsible for ___%

The parties will exchange requests for reimbursement every six months, between May 1-15 and between November 1-15 each year. During those time periods, a parent requesting reimbursement for any child-related items will submit the attached form (see Exhibit A) with a listing of all requested reimbursements for that time period. Along with this form, the requesting parent will include all documentation (receipts, statements) showing evidence for the requested reimbursement.

If the documentation shows that the requested amount was paid, no additional proof of payment needs to be submitted. If an invoice submitted simply shows an amount due, the requesting parent needs to also submit documentation showing that the amount was paid (credit card or Zelle receipt, canceled check, bank printout showing payment, etc.). If a parent fails to submit backup documentation for a requested reimbursement, that reimbursement request is not considered complete and will need to be resubmitted during the next reimbursement period.

Upon receiving the other parent's reimbursement request, a parent will respond within 15 days by either (a) paying the amount requested as reimbursement, or (b) submitting questions about a requested item with a request for more information or a statement that the submitted item is not a reimbursable expense.

Each parent is required to make payment of all non-contested items within 15 days of receipt of the reimbursement request, even if other items on that list are contested or disputed.

If, after requesting additional information about a reimbursement request, the parties still do not agree that a given item is reimbursable, the parent requesting reimbursement may escalate the matter to binding arbitration.

Neither parent will submit reimbursement requests to the other parent outside of the two time periods specified above.

As with most co-parenting issues, communication is important. Do not ignore communication about requested reimbursement, ask for more information when you need it, and state your requests or objections clearly and in a businesslike way. Most importantly, make sure that the child's activities and medical care are not delayed or affected by a failure to reimburse or get these items paid for.

CHAPTER 17

Dispute Resolution

Dispute resolution involves different procedures, all of which are designed to allow the parents to resolve their differences without going to trial and giving up their issues to a judge's decision. It's important that a Parenting Plan addresses methods of dispute resolution that the parents will use in case they can't agree on certain items.

Mediation

The best-known dispute resolution process is probably mediation. Mediations are handled in many ways, but often a mediator will meet with the parents either together or separately, discuss the disputed issues, discuss each parent's position about how the issues should be resolved, and try to bring the parents to common ground. These mediation sessions may or may not include attorneys, but parents are encouraged to have an attorney review their agreements before they are finalized. If either parent is uncomfortable with being in the same room as the other parent during discussions, the mediator can shuttle between private rooms and talk with each parent separately. In some jurisdictions, local or regional laws may provide that mediation discussions are confidential.

Many mediations are now conducted remotely (Zoom, etc.), which permits the mediator and the parents to be in different locations with the ease of using breakout rooms for confidentiality. Zoom mediation generally saves money for both parents and often creates a more relaxed atmosphere, as the parents can remain in a location they're familiar with during the entire process.

Arbitration

Another type of dispute resolution is arbitration, where the parents agree on and the court appoints an arbitrator (who may be an attorney with substantial experience in their type of dispute) who makes the final decision instead of going to trial with a judge. The arbitration ruling is generally final and binding so that neither party can appeal the decision. The arbitration process is generally faster, less formal, and more streamlined than a trial, which permits the parties faster resolution. You may note that in the Reimbursements section in Chapter 16, we suggest that if the parents can't agree on whether a child-related item is reimbursable by one parent to the other, the parents take that issue to an arbitrator. An arbitration resolution will be faster and less expensive than taking that issue to a judge, and getting that issue resolved quickly is best for the child.

Parenting Coordinator

Having a court-ordered PC is another kind of dispute resolution that involves much of what mediation and arbitration do. Parenting coordination was discussed in Chapter 3. When the parents find themselves with frequent disputes and going back to court too often, we strongly suggest looking into having a PC.

When Domestic Violence Is Involved

Cases involving domestic violence (whether an Order of Protection is in effect) need special consideration when it comes to dispute resolution. Many forms of mediation are not appropriate for domestic violence cases, and where mediation is being considered, extensive screening for domestic violence is crucial. Even mediation done via Zoom, where the parties are not in the same room and do not see each other on-screen, can be problematic for domestic violence victims.

ABBREVIATIONS

5/2/2/5 schedule	Type of equal timesharing Parenting Plan
2/2/3 schedule	Type of equal timesharing Parenting Plan
CP	Custodial Parent
DV/IPV	Domestic Violence/Intimate Partner Violence
FROR	First Right of Refusal (first right of caretaking)
JLDM	Joint Legal Decision-Making
LDM	Legal Decision-Making (also called "custody")
NCP	Non-Custodial Parent
PC	Parenting Coordinator
PCCP	Parent-Child Contact Problems
PT	Parenting Time
OOP	Order of Protection

RECOMMENDED READING, APPS, AND WEBSITES

Custody & Co-Parenting During or After Divorce or Separation

Title	Author(s)	Focus
BIFF for Co-Parent Communication: Your Guide to Difficult Texts, Emails, and Social Media Meltdowns	Bill Eddy, LCSW, Esq.; Annette T. Burns, JD; Kevin Chafin, LPC	Email communication
Don't Alienate the Kids: Raising Resilient Children While Avoiding High-Conflict Divorce	Bill Eddy, LCSW, Esq.	Alienation/resistance/refusal
CoParenting after Divorce: A GPS for Healthy Kids	Debra K. Carter, PhD	Court procedure and conflict resolution
Holding Tight/Letting Go: Raising Healthy Kids in Anxious Times	Benjamin D. Garber, PhD	Parenting/co-parenting
Overcoming the Alienation Crisis: 33 Co-parenting Solutions	John Moran, PhD, Shawn McCall, PsyD, & Matthew Sullivan, PhD	Alienation
The Truth about Children and Divorce	Robert Emory, PhD	Children's emotions
A Parent's Guide to Understanding the Effects of Conflict and Divorce	Joan McWilliams, Esq.	Adverse Childhood Experiences (ACEs)
Overcoming Parent-Child Contact Problems	Abigail M. Judge. PhD & Robin M. Deutsch, PhD, ABPP	Alienation

Title	Author(s)	Focus
Parenting after Divorce	Philip M. Stahl, PhD	Resolving conflict
Joint Custody with a Jerk	Julie Ross, M.A. & Judy Corcoran	Uncooperative parents
High Conflict Custody Battle	Amy J.L. Baker, PhD & Paul R. Fine, LCSW	Alienation
Overcoming the Co-parenting Trap: Essential Skills when a Child Resists a Parent	John A. Moran, PhD	Alienation/resistance
How to Talk to Your Children about Divorce	Jill Jones-Soderman, MSW & Allison Quattrocchi	Communicating with child
Calming Upset People with EAR	Bill Eddy, LCSW, Esq.	De-escalation techniques

Dealing with Difficult People and Mental Illness

Title	Author(s)	Focus
Stop Walking on Eggshells	Randi Kreger & Paul Mason, MS	Borderline personality disorder
The Big Book on Borderline Personality Disorder	Shehrina Rooney	Borderline personality disorder
High Conflict People in Legal Disputes	Bill Eddy, LCSW, Esq.	High-conflict personalities
It's All Your Fault: 12 Tips for Managing People who Blame Others for Everything	Bill Eddy, LCSW, Esq.	High-conflict personalities

Title	Author(s)	Focus
The 5 Types of People Who Can Ruin Your Life	Bill Eddy, LCSW, Esq.	High-conflict personalities
The High-Conflict Co-parenting Survial Guide	Andrea LaRochelle, RFM & Megan Hunter, MBA	Self-care
Divorce Poison: How to Protect Your Family from Bad-mouthing and Brainwashing	Richard Warshak, PhD	Preventing alienation
The Sociopath Next Door	Martha Stout, PhD	Antisocials/sociopaths
The Family Law Professional's Field Guide to High-Conflict Litigation: Dynamics, Not Diagnoses	Benjamin Garber, PhD, Dana Prescott, PhD, and Chris Mulchay, PhD	For legal professionals
Mending Fences: A Collaborative, Cognitive Behavioral Reunification Protocol Serving the Best Interests of the Post-Divorce, Polarized Child	Benjamin D. Garber, PhD	For professionals

Handling Divorce

Title	Author(s)	Focus
Crazy Time: Surviving Divorce and Building a New Life	Abigail Tratford	Divorce
The Wiser Divorce	Angela Hallier, JD	Divorce
The Good Divorce	Constance Ahrons, PhD	Divorce

Title	Author(s)	Focus
Splitting: Protecting Yourself while Divorcing Someone with Narcissistic or Borderline Personality Disorder	Bill Eddy, LCSW, Esq. & Randi Kreger	Divorce
Dinosaurs Divorce: A Guide for Changing Families	Marc Brown & Laurie Krasney Brown	For Kids ages 4-6
Two Homes	Claire Masurel	For Kids ages 2-5
What in the World Do You Do When Your Parents Divorce?	Kate Winchester, J.D. & Roberta Beyer, J.D.	For Kids ages 7 -12

Preparing for Court, Custody Evaluations, and Mediation

Title	Author(s)	Focus
Getting to Yes: Negotiating Agreement Without Giving In	Roger Fisher, William Ury, & Bruce Patton	Mediation
Getting Past No: Negotiating in Difficult Situations	William Ury	Mediation
Custody Evaluation Preparation	Launi Sheldon, JD	Custody evaluations
New Ways for Families Pre-Mediation Workbook	Bill Eddy, LCSW, Esq.	Pre-mediation preparation

General Parenting or Relationship Books

Title	Author(s)
The Four Agreements	Don Miguel Ruiz
Parenting with Love & Logic	Foster Cline, MD & Jim Fay
The Whole Brain Child	Daniel Goleman, PhD
The 5 Love Languages	Gary Chapman
Bloom: 50 Things to Say, Think, and Do with Anxious, Angry, and Over-the-Top Kids	Lynne Kenney, PsyD & Wendy Young, LMSW, BCD
The Healthy Parent's ABC's	Benjamin D. Garber, PhD
Caught in the Middle	Benjamin D. Garber, PhD
Taming the Beast	Benjamin D. Garber, PhD

Parenting Communication Apps

https://appclose.com	*https://www.ourfamilywizard.com*
https://coparenter.com/	*https://www.propercomm.com/*
https://divvito.com/	*https://talkingparents.com/home*
https://www.fayr.com/	*https://www.2houses.com/en/*

Alcohol Monitoring Device Websites

Sober Link	https://www.soberlink.com/
BACtrack	https://www.bactrack.com/

Parent Education and High-Conflict Parenting Programs

ORGANIZATION	WEB ADDRESS
Center for Divorce Education	https://divorce-education.com/
Children in Between Online	https://divorce-education.com/
High Conflict Institute Conflict Influencer™ Class	https://www.highconflicttraining.com/ conflict-influencer-all
High Conflict Institute New Ways 4 Families® Class + Coaching	https://www.highconflicttraining.com/ coaching-nwff
FIT (Families in Transition)	https://www.ncsc.org/consulting- and-research/areas-of-expertise/ children-and-families/cady-initiative/ complex-cases/families-in-transition
New Beginnings	https://divorceandparenting.com/
Parent Universities	https://www.parentuniversities.com/ high-conflict-class.html
In-person classes in your community or offered by your court system	

Addiction Resources

Al-Anon	https://al-anon.org/
Alcoholics Anonymous	https://www.aa.org/
Nar-Anon	https://www.nar-anon.org/
SAMSHA (Substantive Abuse and Mental Health Services Administration)	https://www.samhsa.gov/find-help/national-helpline
SMART Recovery	https://smartrecovery.org/

SAMPLE HOLIDAY PLAN CHART

NOTE: These are suggestions. Parents are free to modify the definition of holidays (or delete certain holidays) to fit their particular situation. Please see the discussion of many holidays in Chapter 5.

Sample Holiday Plan

Holiday	Parent A	Parent B	Description
Easter Sunday	Odd	Even	From Friday 3 pm (or after school) until the following Monday morning at 8 am (or return to school).
Spring Break	Odd	Even	Defined as the actual days off of school, plus the assigned parent's regular weekend; spring break may run from the time school is out until the following Friday (5 pm) or may start on Monday morning at 8 am and run to the following Monday (end of break) with the child's return to school
July 4th	n/a	n/a	Regular Parenting Time Schedule
Fall Break	Even	Odd	If Fall Break is a week: Defined as the actual days off from school, plus the assigned parent's regular weekend; spring break may run from the time school is out until the following Friday (5 pm); or may start on Monday morning at 8 am and run to the following Monday (end of break) with the child's return to school. If fall break is less than a full week, the parents will follow the regular parenting time schedule.

Holiday	Parent A	Parent B	Description
Halloween	Even	Odd	Until the child is 13 years old: from release from school on Halloween (or 3 pm if a non-school day) until November 1 at return to school (or 8 am if a non-school day). When the child is 13 and older, Halloween is no longer a designated holiday.
Thanksgiving	Odd	Even	From Wednesday after school (3 pm if school is not in session on Wednesday) until return to school on the Monday after the holiday (8 am if a non-school day). If the school takes off earlier than Wednesday, the regular parenting time schedule remains in effect until Wednesday.
Christmas Eve	Even	Odd	12/24 at 9 am until 12/25 at 9 am
Christmas Day	Odd	Even	12/25 at 9 am until 12/26 at 9 am
Winter Break	First half – Even Second half – Odd	First half – Odd Second half – Even	The parents will exchange the child at noon on the day that is mid-way through the break. The break period is defined as beginning with release of school on the last day before break and ending at the return to school after break. If there are an odd number of days in the break, the parent with second half gets the additional overnight.
New Year's Eve & Day	n/a	n/a	Not a separate holiday – included in winter break.
Child's Birthday			Each parent will celebrate the child's birthday during their parenting time closest to the birthday.
Parent Birthday	n/a	n/a	Each parent will celebrate with the child during regular parenting time.

Holiday	Parent A	Parent B	Description
Mother's Day	Every year		Beginning Saturday at 3 pm and ending Monday 8 am (or return to school).
Father's Day		Every year	Beginning Saturday at 3 pm and ending Monday 8 am (or return to school).
MLK Day, Memorial Day	Even	Odd	Beginning at the end of school on Friday (3 pm if a non-school day) and ending with return to school on Tuesday (8 am if a non-school day).
Presidents' Day, Labor Day	Odd	Even	
Other school or federal holidays			Regular Parenting Time Schedule

SAMPLE TECHNOLOGY AGREEMENT

Co-parent Technology/Media Agreement

This Agreement for the use of technology and other media has been made by _____ and _____ on (date) _____. The parties agree to follow this Agreement and will individually/jointly review this agreement with the child(ren). This Agreement will be periodically reviewed and updated as the needs of the children change and new technology becomes available and/or appropriate.

A. Defining Devices

At this time, technology devices utilized by the kids, and subject to this agreement, include 1) (e.g., cell phone, the two iPads) at _____'s house and 2) (e.g., the Amazon "kindles") at _____'s house.

The following technology devices are not subject to this agreement:

_____

B. Terms of Agreement

1. The parents agree that the children will have no unsupervised access to the internet.

2. The parents agree that the children will not be allowed to download or play games with platforms that allow them to play with strangers or enter chat rooms.

3. The parents agree that the children will not be allowed to download or use any social media apps without the approval of both parents.

OR

   The parents agree that the child(ren) may download and use the following social media apps: _____. Any additional apps must be approved by both parents.

4. The children will not be allowed to download _____ on their devices.

5. The parents agree to the following parental controls:

    _____.

6. Parameters for screen time are as follows:

    No more than _____ on weekdays.

    No more than _____on weekend days.

*The parents agree that there may be exceptions to these parameters on days when the children are home sick, have a snow day, etc.

* The parents agree that family movies and other screen-related activities with parents are not subject to these parameters.

7. The parents agree to use **commonsensemedia.com** to determine the age-appropriateness of games, apps, movies, and shows. If a parent wishes to allow a child to view media beyond the age recommended by commonsensemedia, they will seek permission of the other parent.

8. The parents agree to make sure that devices are turned in each night and placed in a secure location by _____PM.

9. The parents agree to monitor the children's devices frequently, such as checking their search histories.

10. All login information to any shared devices will be provided to both parents.

11. Parental agreement is required for the addition of any technological devices or changes to this agreement.

NAME: _____

DATE: _____

NAME: _____

DATE: _____

NOTES

CHAPTER 1

1. M. E. Feinberg, "The Internal Structure and Ecological Context of Co-parenting: A Framework for Research and Intervention," *Parenting* 3 (2003): 95-131, https://www.ncbi.nlm.nih.gov/pmc/articles/PMC3185375/.

2. C. R. Ahrons and R. H. Rodgers, Divorced Families: A Multidisciplinary Developmental View (Norton, 1987); E. E. Maccoby, R. H. Mnookin, C. E. Depner and H. E. Peters, *Dividing the Child: Social and Legal Dilemmas of Custody* (Harvard University Press, 1987).

3. Matthew Sullivan, "Co-parenting and the Parenting Coordination Process," *Journal of Child Custody* 5, (2008).

4. Milfred D. Dale, Delores Bomrad, and Alexander Jones, "Parenting Coordination Law in the U.S. and Canada: A Review," *Family Court Review* 58, no. 3 (2020), https://doi.org/10.1111/fcre.12507.

5. Michael Saini, Robin Belcher-Timme and Daniel Nau, "A Multidisciplinary Perspective on the Role, Functions, and Effectiveness of Parenting Coordination," *Family Court Review* 68, no. 3 (2020): 658-72, https://doi.org/10.1111/fcre.12506.

CHAPTER 2

6. William G. Austin, Linda Fieldstone and Marsha Kline Pruett, "Bench Book for Assessing Parental Gatekeeping in Parenting Disputes: Understanding the Dynamics of Gate Closing and Opening for the Best Interests of Children," *Journal of Child Custody* 10, no. 1 (2013): 1-16, https://doi.org/10.1080/15379 418.2013.778693.

7. William G. Austin, L. Fieldstone and M. K. Pruett, "Bench Book for Assessing Parental Gatekeeping in Parenting Disputes: Understanding the Dynamics of Gate Closing and Opening for the Best Interests of Children," *Journal of Child Custody* 10, no. 1 (2013): 1-16, https://doi.org/10.1080/15379418.2013.778693

8. Austin, Fieldstone and Pruett, "Bench Book."

9. M. R. Dadds, E. Atkinson, C. Turner, G. J. Blums and B. Lendich, "Family Conflict and Child Adjustment: Evidence for a Cognitive-Contextual Model of Intergenerational Transmission," *Journal of Family Psychology* 13, no. 2 (1999): 194-208; E. M. Cummings and P. T. Davies, *Marital Conflict and Children: An Emotional Security Perspective* (Guilford Press, 2001).

10. P. R. Amato and T. D. Afifi, "Feeling Caught Between Parents: Adult Children's Relations with Parents and Subjective Well-Being," *Journal of Marriage and Family* 68, (2006): 222–235; Cheryl Buehler and Deborah Welsh, "A Process Model of Adolescents' Triangulation into Parents' Marital Conflict: The Role of Emotional Reactivity," *Journal of Family Psychology* 23, no. 2 (2009):167–180, https://doi.org/10.1037/a0014976.

11. Jenna R. Shimkowski and Paul Schrodt, "Coparental Communication as a Mediator of Interparental Conflict and Young Adult Children's Mental Well-Be-

ing," *Communication Monographs* 79, no. 1 (2012): 48-71, https://www.tand-fonline.com/doi/abs/10.1080/03637751.2011.646492ment; Amato and Afifi, "Feeling Caught between Parents."

12. G. M. Fosco and J. H. Grych, "Adolescent Triangulation into Parental Conflicts: Longitudinal Implications for Appraisals and Adolescent-Parent Relations," Journal of Marriage and Family 72 (2010): 254-266, https://doi.org/10.1111/j.1741-3737.2010.00697.x.

13. Richard Warshak, Divorce Poison (William Morrow Publishing, 2011).

14. M. G. Walters and S. Friedlander, "When a Child Rejects a Parent: Working with the Intractable Resist/Refuse Dynamic," *Family Court Review* 54, no. 3 (2016): 424-445. https://doi.org/10.1111/fcre.12238.

15. [1] PA as a "syndrome" under the Diagnostic and Statistical Manual (DSM) has been rejected by the American Psychiatric Association (2022), but the presence of its dynamics in some separated family relationships is well documented.

16. J. B. Kelly and J. R. Johnston, "The Alienated Child: A Reformulation of Parental Alienation Syndrome." *Family Court Review* 39, no. 3 (2001):249-266.

17. E. N. Neger and R. J. Prinz, "Interventions to Address Parenting and Parental Substance Abuse: Conceptual and Methodological Considerations," *Clinical Psychology Review* 39, (2015): 71-82, https://doi.org/10.1016/j.cpr.2015.04.004.

18. L. Lander, J. Howsare and M. Byrne, "The Impact of Substance Use Disorders on Families and Children: From Theory to Practice," *Social Work in Public Health* 28, nos. 3-4 (2013): 194-205, https://doi.org/10.1080/19371918.2013.759005.

19. "What Is Domestic Abuse," COVID-19 Response, United Nations, accessed October 16, 2024, https://www.un.org/en/coronavirus/what-is-domestic-abuse.

20. "Domestic Violence," United States Department of Justice Office on Violence Against Women, accessed October 16, 2024, https://www.justice.gov/ovw/domestic-violence#:~:text=Domestic%20violence%20is%20a%20pattern,-control%20over%20another%20intimate%20partner.

21. Nancy Ver Steegh and Claire Dalton, "Report from the Wingspread Conference on Domestic Violence and Family Courts," *Family Court Review* 46, no. 3 (2008):463-464.

22. Ver Steegh and Dalton, "Report."

23. Ver Steegh and Dalton, "Report."

24. P. R. Amato and B. Keith, "Parental Divorce and the Well-being of Children: A Meta-Analysis," *Psychological Bulletin* 110, no. 1 (1991): 26-46.

25. M. R. Dadds, E. Atkinson, C. Turner, G. J. Blums, and B. Lendich, "Family Conflict and Child Adjustment: Evidence for a Cognitive-Contextual Model of Intergenerational Transmission," *Journal of Family Psychology* 13, (1999): 194-208; E. M. Cummings and P. T. Davies, *Marital Conflict and Children: An Emotional Security Perspective* (Guilford Press, 2001). J. Rowen and R. E. Em-

ery, "Parental Denigration: Examining the Deliberate Denigration of Co-parents as Reported by Young Adults and Its Association with Parent-Child Closeness," *Couple and Family Psychology: Research and Practice* 3, no. 3 (2014): 165-177; Joan B. Kelly and Robert E. Emery, "Children's Adjustment Following Divorce: Risk and Resilience Perspectives," *Family Relations* 52, no. 4 (2003): 352-362; See also Amato and Keith, "Parental Divorce."

26. Rowen and Emery, "Parental Denigration"; J. Grych, M. Seid and F. A. Fincham, "Assessing Marital Conflict from the Child's Perspective: The Children's Perception of Interparental Conflict Scale," Child Development 63 (1992): 558-573.

27. C. Buehler and D. P. Welsh, "A Process Model of Adolescents' Triangulation into Parents' Marital Conflict: The Role of Emotional Reactivity," *Journal of Family Psychology* 23, no. 2 (2009): 167-180.

28. J. I. Zimic, V. Jakic, "Familial Risk Factors Favoring Drug Addiction Onset," *Journal of Psychoactive Drugs* 44, no. 2 (2012): 173-185; See also A. Barrett and R. Turner, "Family Structure and Substance Use Problems in Adolescence and Early Adulthood: Examining Explanations for the Relationship," *Addiction* 101, no. 1 (2006):109-120. https://doi.org/10.1111/j.1360-0443.2005.01296.x

29. I. K. Gilbert, M. J. Breiding, M. T. Merrick, W. W. Thompson, D.C. Ford, S.S. Dhingra and S.E. Parks, "Childhood Adversity and Adult Chronic Disease: An Update from Ten States and the District of Columbia, 2010," *American Journal of Preventive Medicine* 48, no. 3 (2015):345-9. https://doi.org/10.1016/j.amepre.2014.09.006.

30. "Effects of Domestic Violence on Children," Office on Women's Health, U.S. Department of Health and Human Services, last updated February 15, 2021, https://www.womenshealth.gov/relationships-and-safety/domestic-violence/effects-domestic-violence-children

31. "Effects of Domestic Violence on Children," Office on Women's Health.

32. Daniel S. Shaw and Robert E. Emery, "Parental Conflict and Other Correlates of the Adjustment of School Aged Children Whose Parents Have Separated," *Journal of Abnormal Child Psychology* 15 (1987): 269-281.

CHAPTER 3

33. Sullivan, "Co-parenting and the Parenting Coordination Process."

34. Philip Stahl, Parenting after Divorce (Impact Publishers, 2007).

35. E. M. Hetherington and M. M. Stanley-Hagan, "Parenting in Divorced and Remarried Families," In *Handbook of Parenting, Vol. 3. Status and Social Conditions of Parenting,* ed. M. H. Bornstein (Lawrence Erlbaum Associates, 1995), 233-54.

36. Sullivan, "Co-parenting and the Parenting Coordination Process."

37. Joan Kelly, "Children's Adjustment in Conflicted Marriage and Divorce: A Decade Review of Research," *Journal of the American Academy of Child and Adolescent Psychiatry* 39, no. 8 (2000): 963-73.

38. Kelly, "Children's Adjustment."

CHAPTER 4

39. Bill Eddy, Annette T. Burns and Kevin Chafin, *BIFF for Co-Parent Communication* (Unhooked Media, 2020), https://www.unhookedmedia.com/stock/p/biff-for-coparents.

CHAPTER 5

40. It's strongly advised that the parents not try to reach "exactly" equal parenting time schedules. It's not possible. Your child is not a timeshare, and the natural flow of a calendar year (including holidays, vacations, non-school days, 3-day weekends, sick days, etc.) is not compatible with having exactly equal parenting time. We will strive to use "relatively equal" throughout this book.

41. We will use the term "breastfeeding" to indicate both breastfeeding and chestfeeding.

42. Linda Nielsen, "Shared Parenting After Divorce: A Review of Shared Residential Parenting Research," *Journal of Divorce and Remarriage* 52 (2011): 586-609.

43. L. Lander, J. Howsare, M. Byrne, "The Impact of Substance Use Disorders on Families and Children: From Theory to Practice," *Social Work in Public Health* 28, nos. 3-4 (2013): 194-205. https://doi.org/10.1080/19371918.2013.759005.

44. The reason for this provision is to prevent a parent from taking individual days as "vacation" days, simply to deprive the other parent of the most parenting days as possible.

CHAPTER 13

45. Isabela Reed, *Navigating the Digital Age: A Parent's Guide to Raising Teens in the World of Social Media* (Independently Published, 2023).

CHAPTER 15

46. Note that the authors are not saying this is the right thing to do, but it does often happen.

47. Gabrielle Davis, Loretta Frederick and Nancy Ver Steegh, *Practice Guides for Family Court Decision-Making in Domestic Abuse-Related Child Custody Matters* (Battered Women's Justice Project, 2018), https://bwjp.org/assets/compiled-practice-guides-may-2018.pdf.

ACKNOWLEDGMENTS

The authors would like to acknowledge the many contributions of family law organizations that consistently seek to better the lives of children and parents in the family court system despite the system's drawbacks. Those organizations include the Association of Family and Conciliation Courts (AFCC), including the Arizona Chapter of AFCC; the American Academy of Matrimonial Lawyers (AAML); the National Council of Juvenile and Family Court Judges (NCJFCJ); the Maricopa County Bar Association Family Law Section; the State Bar of Arizona Family Law Section; and our many mentors and colleagues who have guided us through the family court maze.

We also acknowledge every member of CoS. You know who you are and what you've added to our professional lives over the last decade.

Annette Burns

It's impossible to acknowledge all of the mentors, friends, colleagues, and family support I've received over my forty years of practicing law, but I will try:

- To my husband Jim and my beautiful, talented daughters: Thank you for always being there.

- To my co-author Nicole: This book wouldn't exist without you pushing and inspiring me.

- To my many legal mentors, Rad, Ed, John (and many others): You were always there when I needed you as a baby attorney.

- To Megan, the Hub of the Wheel: Thank you!

- To Peter, whose leadership at AFCC always inspired me.

- To Bill Eddy, a constant inspiration.

Nicole Siqueiros-Stoutner

- To my daughter: Your beauty, joy, and curiosity remind me of the wonder in the world and give my life purpose.

- To my husband: Your steadfast love and partnership mean more to me than words can express. I love you and our life together.

- To my wonderful parents, who mean so much to me and are my guiding lights: Your endless wisdom and encouragement are the foundation of everything I do.

- To my best friend, Katie: Thank you for always being there for me and being the best cinnamon roll sister I could ever hope to have.

- To Tiffany: Thirty years of friendship and laughter have been a true gift.

- To my co-author, Annette Burns: Your dedication and expertise made this book possible. I am so grateful to have you in my life.

- To Megan, for your hard work: Thank you!

- To all those who mentored me, inspired me, and encouraged me on this journey, especially Lura, Jeff, Sherry, Ken F., Launi, Angie H., Mervyn, Lisa, Jenny G., and many others whose support has been invaluable.

THE AUTHORS

Annette Burns, JD, is an attorney and a certified Family Law Specialist and Parenting Coordinator practicing in Arizona. She is a past president of the international interdisciplinary organization, the Association of Family and Conciliation Courts (AFCC), a nonprofit organization of over 5000 international family law related professionals. She is a former Fellow of the American Academy of Matrimonial Lawyers (AAML), a national organization composed of the nation's top attorneys. She has been named a Super Lawyer every year from 2007-2023 and has been named in Super Lawyers' Arizona's Top Female Attorneys and Top Attorneys several times. She is the co-author of *BIFF for Co-Parent Communication* with high-conflict expert Bill Eddy, LCSW, Esq. and co-parenting expert, Kevin Chafin, LPC., and co-authored the chapter on Parenting Coordination in *Family Dispute Resolution: Process and Practice Handbook* (Oxford Press). Her private practice in Arizona focuses on family law. Annette lives in Scottsdale, Arizona.

Nicole Siqueiros-Stoutner, JD, is an award-winning jurist, mediator, former judicial officer, and court-appointed Parenting Coordinator. Her early career included roles with Child Protective Services and a domestic violence shelter before transitioning to family law practice and serving a year as a full-time judicial officer in the Superior Court of Maricopa County, Arizona. Nicole is a partner at her law firm in Scottsdale, Arizona. She has served on the Board of Directors for the Maricopa County Bar Association's Family Law Committee and the Los Abogados Hispanic Bar Association. She currently serves on the Arizona State Bar Family Law Executive Council. Nicole was named an Arizona Super Lawyer in 2024 and an Arizona Rising Star from 2017 to 2020 by Thomson Reuters. In 2011, she was honored as one of Arizona's "Forty Under 40" community leaders by the *Phoenix Business Journal*. Nicole frequently writes and lectures on various topics, including family law litigation and procedure, cultural competency, mental health, and the prevention of domestic violence. In her spare time, she enjoys spending time with her family and traveling.